917.95   Grabowski, John F.
G   The Northwest

TALCOTT SCHOOL
1840 W. Ohio St. (22)

STATE REPORTS

The Northwest

ALASKA ★ IDAHO ★ OREGON ★ WASHINGTON

By
John F. Grabowski
Patricia A. Grabowski

CHELSEA HOUSE PUBLISHERS
New York   Philadelphia

Produced by James Charlton Associates
New York, New York.

Copyright © 1992 by Chelsea House Publishers, a division of Main Line Book Co.
All rights reserved. Printed and bound in the United States of America.

    3   5   7   9   8   6   4   2

No part of this book may be reproduced or utilized in any form, or by any means, electronic or mechanical, including photocopying, recording, or by any information storage or retrieval system, without permission in writing from the publisher.

Library of Congress Cataloging-in-Publication Data

Grabowski, John F.
    The Northwest : Alaska, Idaho, Oregon, Washington / by
John Grabowski, Patricia Grabowski.
    p. cm. — (State reports)
    Includes bibliographical references and index.
    Summary: Discusses the geographical, historical, and cultural aspects of Alaska, Idaho, Oregon, and Washington.
    ISBN 0-7910-1051-1
        0-7910-1398-7 (pbk.)
    1. Northwest, Pacific—Juvenile literature. 2. Alaska—Juvenile literature. [1. Northwest, Pacific. 2. Alaska. 3. Idaho. 4. Oregon. 5. Washington (State)] I. Grabowski, Patricia. II. Title. III. Series: Aylesworth, Thomas G. State reports.

F852.3.G73 1992   91-30782
917.95—dc20   CIP
                                             AC

Contents

Alaska

State Seal, **5**; State Flag and Motto, **7**; State Capital, **9**; State Name and Nicknames, **10**; State Flower, Tree, Bird, Fish, Gem, Marine Mammal, Mineral, Sport and Song, **10**; Population, **10**; Geography and Climate, **11**; Industries, **11**; Agriculture, **11**; Government, **12**; History, **12**; Sports, **14**; Major Cities, **14**; Places to Visit, **15**; Events, **17**; Famous People, **18**; Colleges and Universities, **18**; Where to Get More Information, **18**.

Idaho

State Seal, **19**; State Flag and Motto, **21**; State Capital, **21**; State Name and Nickname, **24**; State Flower, Tree, Bird, Gem, Horse and Song, **24**; Population, **24**; Geography and Climate, **24**; Industries, **25**; Agriculture, **25**; Government, **25**; History, **25**; Sports, **27**; Major Cities, **27**; Places to Visit, **27**; Events, **28**; Famous People, **29**; Where to Get More Information, **30**.

Oregon

State Seal, **31**; State Flag and Motto, **33**; State Capital, **35**; State Name and Nicknames, **36**; State Flower, Tree, Bird, Animal, Dance, Fish, Gemstone and Hostess, **36**; State Insect, Rock and Song, **37**; Population, **37**; Geography and Climate, **37**; Industries, **37**; Agriculture, **37**; Government, **38**; History, **38**; Sports, **40**; Major Cities, **41**; Places to Visit, **41**; Events, **42**; Famous People, **44**; Colleges and Universities, **46**; Where to Get More Information, **46**.

Washington

State Seal, **47**; State Flag and Motto, **49**; State Capital, **51**; State Name and Nickname, **52**; State Flower, Tree, Bird, Dance, Fish, Gem and Song, **52**; Population, **52**; Geography and Climate, **52**; Industries, **53**; Agriculture, **53**; Government, **53**; History, **54**; Sports, **55**; Major Cities **56**; Places to Visit, **57**; Events, **58**; Famous People, **59**; Colleges and Universities, **61**; Where to Get More Information, **61**.

Bibliography 62

Index 63

Alaska

The state seal of the territory of Alaska was adopted in 1913. On the present seal, adopted in 1959, "state" was substituted for "territory." Pictured in the center are icebergs; railroads; forests; ships; native people; and symbols for mining, agriculture, fisheries, and fur seal rookeries. The northern lights shine above them, with "The Seal of the State of Alaska" printed in a circle surrounding the seal.

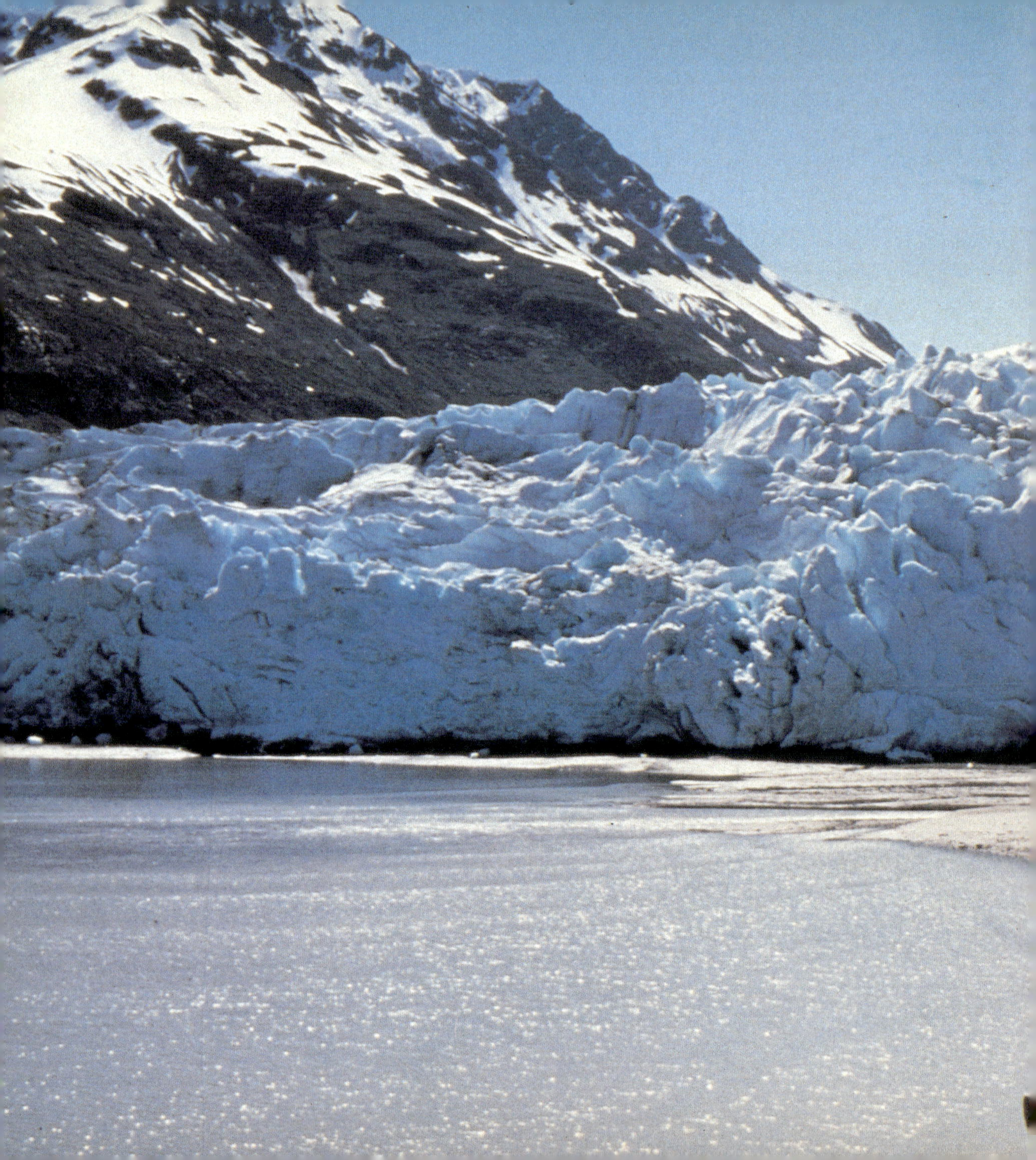

State Flag

In 1926, a contest to design a territorial flag was held among Alaska's schoolchildren. The winning design, submitted by 13-year-old Benny Benson, was adopted in 1927. The blue field stands for the Alaskan sky and fields of forget-me-nots; the seven gold stars forming the Big Dipper represent Alaska's gold mines; and the eighth star—the North Star—symbolizes Alaska's northernmost location. It was designated state flag in 1959.

State Motto
North to the Future

This phrase was adopted as the official state motto in 1967. It was chosen from among 761 entries in a competition won by Juneau newsman Richard Peter.

When George Vancouver was exploring the Alaskan coast in 1794, Glacier Bay was still occupied by a glacier.

State Capital
Cities or towns
OF SPECIAL INTEREST
RUSSIA
Penzhin Bay
Chukchi Sea
Barrow
Kotzebue Sound
Kotzebue
Anadyr Gulf
Bering Strait
RUSSIA (U.S.S.R.)
UNITED STATES
Nome
Norton Sound
ALASKA
N
INTERNATIONAL DATELINE
BERING SEA
Bristol Bay
ALASKA PENINSULA
ALEUTIAN ISLANDS
PACIFIC OCEAN
Distance scale
0 50 100 200 300 400 500 600 700 800 900 1000 Miles
0 50 100 200 300 400 500 600 700 800 900 1000 1100 1200 1300 1400 1500 1600 Kilometres

The Alaska State Capitol in Juneau is built from brick and limestone and has pillars of Alaskan marble.

State Capital

Juneau has been the capital of Alaska since it became a territory of the United States in 1912. Construction began on the six-story capitol building in 1929 and was completed in 1931. The total construction cost, including land, was about $1 million. Tokeen marble from Alaska was used for the four Doric columns of the portico and for the interior trim.

State Name and Nicknames

The name Alaska is taken from the word *alakshak*, used by the people of the Aleutian Islands to mean "mainland." After the United States bought Alaska from Russia in 1867, the name was applied to the territory and then to the state.

Although Alaska has no official nickname, it is often referred to as *Seward's Folly* or *Seward's Ice Box* because it was purchased for the United States by Secretary of State William Seward. Other nicknames include *Land of the Midnight Sun* and *The Last Frontier*.

State Flower

The forget-me-not, *Myosotis alpestris*, was adopted state flower and floral emblem by the legislature in 1949.

State Tree

In 1962, the Sitka spruce, *Picea sitchensis*, was adopted state tree.

State Bird

The willow ptarmigan,

Forget-me-nots, the state flower of Alaska.

Lagopus lagopus alascensis Swarth, was chosen state bird in 1955.

State Fish

In 1963, the King salmon, *Oncorhynchus tshawytscha*, was named state fish.

State Gem

Jade was selected state gem in 1968.

State Marine Mammal

In 1983, the bowhead whale, also known as the right whale, was chosen state marine mammal.

State Mineral

The state legislature designated gold as the state mineral in 1968.

State Sport

Dog mushing, once an important means of transportation, was named the official state sport in 1972.

State Song

"Alaska's Flag," with words by Marie Drake and music by Elinor Dusenbury, was adopted as state song in 1955.

Population

The population of Alaska in 1990 was 551,947 making it the 49th most populous state. There are 0.9 people per square mile—64.3 percent of the population live in towns and cities. About one-third of the people were born in the state.

The state bird of Alaska is the ptarmigan.

Alaska

Geography and Climate

Bounded on the north by the Arctic Ocean, on the east by Canada (Yukon Territory and British Columbia), on the south by the Pacific Ocean and the Gulf of Alaska, and on the west by the Bering Sea and Bering Strait, Alaska has an area of 591,000 square miles, making it the largest state in the United States. The climate of the southeast, southwest, and central regions is moist and mild, while the far north is extremely dry. Alaska experiences long summer days and long winter nights. The four main land regions include: the Pacific and Arctic mountain systems, the central plateau, and the Arctic Coastal Plain. The highest point in the state—as well as in the United States—is Mount McKinley (20,320 feet), and the lowest point is at sea level along the Pacific Ocean. The major waterways of the state are the Yukon, Koyukuk, Tanana, Kuskokwim, Colville, Noatak, Kobuk, Susitna, Matanuska, Copper, Alsek, Stikine, and Taku rivers. Iliamna Lake, on the Alaska Peninsula, is the largest lake in the state.

Logging is an important industry in Alaska.

Industries

The principal industries of Alaska are oil, gas, tourism, and commercial fishing. The chief manufactured products are fish products, lumber and pulp, and furs.

Agriculture

The chief crops of the state are barley, hay, greenhouse nursery products, potatoes, lettuce, and milk. Alaska is also a livestock state. There are estimated to be 9,500 cattle, 2,400 sheep, 23,000 reindeer, and 6,000 chickens and turkeys on its farms. Spruce, yellow cedar, and hemlock are harvested. Sand and gravel, crushed and broken stone, and gold are important mineral resources. Commercial fishing brings in $1.2 billion per year.

Government

The governor and lieutenant governor, the only elected officials of Alaska, serve four-year terms. Other top executives, including the attorney general and the adjutant general, are appointed by the governor with the approval of the state legislature. The legislature, which meets annually, consists of a 20-member senate and a 40-member house of representatives. Alaska has 14 senatorial districts, six of which elect two senators each, and eight of which elect one each. Of the 27 representative districts, 13 elect two representatives each, and 14 elect one each. Senators serve four-year terms and representatives serve two-year terms. The most recent constitution was adopted in 1956, three years before Alaska became a state. In addition to its two United States senators, Alaska has one representative in the U.S. House of Representatives. The state has three votes in the electoral college.

History

When the first Europeans arrived, Eskimos were living in the coastal areas in the far north and west, Aleuts on the Alaska Peninsula, and Indians, including the Tlingit, Haida, Tsimshian, and Athapaskan tribes, along the southeastern coast and in the interior.

In 1725, Peter the Great of Russia commissioned Vitus Bering, a Danish sea captain, to explore the northwestern coast of the American continent. In 1728, Bering sailed through the strait that now bears his name and proved that the land was part of the North American continent. In 1741, Bering made his second expedition to explore the North Pacific. He sighted Mount Saint Elias on Alaska's southern coast and landed on Kayak Island. Shortly thereafter, Bering died of scurvy, a disease resulting from the lack of vitamin C. Members of the expedition brought sea otter pelts back to Russia, thus giving rise to a large fur trading operation. Other explorers from Spain, England, and France entered Alaskan waters in search of a northwest passage between the Atlantic and Pacific oceans. Among them was Captain James Cook of the British navy, who sailed through the Bering Strait into the Arctic Ocean in 1778, exploring the inlet that was later named for him.

The first permanent Russian settlement was established on Kodiak Island in 1784 by fur trader Gregory Shelikof. In 1799, the Russian government chartered the Russian-American Company, a fur-trading firm, with Alexander Baranof as its manager. In retaliation for his harsh treatment toward them, the Tlingit Indians killed many settlers and destroyed

Alaska

the town of Sitka in 1802. Baranof rebuilt the town in 1804 and continued as its manager until 1817. He died in 1819. Profits from the fur trade declined and the Russians lost interest in Alaska. By the late 1850s, Russia wanted to sell Alaska to the United States. The purchase was finally negotiated by Secretary of State William H. Seward. On March 30, 1867, he paid $7,200,000—less than two cents per acre—for the region. Americans who disapproved of the purchase nicknamed Alaska *Seward's Folly* and *Seward's Ice Box*.

The federal government paid little attention to the newly acquired land until 1880, when Joe Juneau and Richard Harris found gold at the site of present-day Juneau. The arrival of many prospectors prompted Congress to pass the Organic Act of 1884, which provided for a governor and a federal court for the region. With new discoveries of gold on the Klondike River in Canada in 1896 and at Nome in 1899, Alaska's population grew again, increasing the need for a stronger local government. At about the same time, copper mines were established on the Copper River. By 1900, salmon fishing had become an important part of Alaska's economy, with at least 50 canneries in operation..

Alaskan's sent their first nonvoting delegate to Congress in 1906, and the pressing need for more self-government was finally satisfied in 1912, when Congress passed the second Organic Act, granting Alaska territorial status and providing for a legislature.

During the Great Depression of the 1930s, the federal government established a colony of 200 families in the Matanuska

Alaska's Russian heritage is apparent in this Ninilchik church.

The Alaska Pipeline stretches south from Prudhoe Bay for 800 miles along the North American continent.

Valley near Anchorage. This region currently provides most of Alaska's farm products. World War II brought many changes to Alaska. Recognizing the territory's strategic geographical location, the United States government built many military installations there to help defend North America. The Alaska Highway, the only road linking Alaska with the lower 48 states, was built as a supply route for U.S. troops in 1942.

Bills for statehood had been brought before Congress since 1912, but it was not until January 3, 1959, that Alaska was admitted to the Union as the 49th state. In 1968, one of the largest oil fields in the world was discovered at Prudhoe Bay. The 800-mile-long Alaska Pipeline, built to transport the oil from northern Alaska to the port of Valdez, has sparked the economic growth of the state.

Sports

Sporting events on the collegiate and secondary school levels are played throughout the state. In addition, hunting, fishing, skiing, and dogsledding are popular pastimes. The most famous dogsled race, the 1,049-mile Iditarod Trail Race, is held annually in early March.

Major Cities

Anchorage (population 226,700). This modern city, Alaska's largest, sits on a high bluff overlooking Cook Inlet. Originally established as the construction headquarters for the Alaska railroad in 1914, it has become the transportation and business center of south-central Alaska. More than half of the state's residents live in Anchorage.

Alaska

Things to see in Anchorage: Alaska Aviation Heritage Museum, Alaska Public Lands Information Center, Alaska Zoo, Alyeska Resort, Anchorage Museum of History and Art, Chugach State Park, Fort Richardson Fish and Wildlife Center, Heritage Library and Museum, Imaginarium, and Oscar Anderson House (1915).

Fairbanks (population 22,600). Established as a trading post in 1901 by Captain E. T. Barnette, Fairbanks lies near the geographical center of the state. When gold was discovered the following year, the settlement was flooded with prospectors, who named the town after Senator Fairbanks of Indiana. A second growth spurt occurred in 1968, when oil was found in Prudhoe Bay, 390 miles to the north.

Things to see in Fairbanks: Cripple Creek Resort, Gold Dredge Number 8, National Oceanic Atmospheric Administration Satellite Tracking Station, Riverboat Discovery, University of Alaska Museum, Alaskaland, and Mining Valley.

Autumn arrives in Anchorage, Alaska.

Places to Visit

The National Park Service maintains 15 areas in the state of Alaska: Klondike Gold Rush National Historical Park, Sitka National Historical Park, Kenai Fjords National Park, Kobuk Valley National Park, Denali National Park and Preserve, Gates of the Arctic National Park and Preserve, Glacier Bay National Park and Preserve, Katmai National Park and Preserve, Lake Clark National Park and Preserve, Wrangell-St. Elias National Park and Preserve, Noatak National Preserve, Yukon-Charley Rivers National Preserve, Cape Krusenstern National Monument, Admiralty Island National Monument, and Misty Fiords National

Monument. In addition, there are 56 state recreation areas.

Haines: Fort William H. Seward. The first permanent army post in Alaska features a replica of a tribal house, a trapper's cabin, and totem poles.

Homer: Pratt Museum. This museum features Eskimo and Indian artifacts, a botanical garden, and a marine gallery.

Juneau: Alaska State Museum. Exhibits in this museum relate to native art and state history.

Kenai: Fort Kenay Historical Museum. This museum is housed in a replica of the log barracks that were part of a U.S. military post.

Ketchikan: Saxman Native Village. One of the highlights of this Tlingit Indian village is a totem park in which master carvers can be seen at work.

Kodiak: Kodiak National Wildlife Refuge. The refuge, occupying nearly 2 million acres of land, is set aside to preserve the natural habitat of the Kodiak bear, as well as other native animals.

Nome: Carrie McLain Memorial Museum. This museum contains exhibits that depict the city's gold rush years, in addition to displays on Eskimo art and archaeological artifacts.

Palmer: Musk Ox Farm. Guided tours are available on this farm, which is one of the few in the world where musk ox are raised

Petersburg: Clausen Memorial Museum. One of the displays features a world-record, 126½-pound king salmon.

Seward: Resurrection Bay Historical Society Museum. This museum is devoted to displays and artifacts of Alaska's—and Seward's—history.

Sitka: St. Michael's Cathedral. The cathedral contains an extensive collection of Russian orthodox art.

Skagway: Trail of '98 Museum. The museum contains elaborate displays on the cultures of the natives of Alaska.

Soldotna: Kenai National Wildlife Refuge. This refuge, which was established by President Roosevelt in 1941, has its headquarters in Soldotna.

Valdez: Valdez Museum. This museum has displays on the pioneer heritage of the city, in

The Tlingit leave their mark with this tribal house front at Ketchikan, Alaska.

Alaska

addition to exhibits on the Alaska Pipeline.

Wrangell: Wrangell Museum. The museum features displays of Tlingit Indian artifacts among its many exhibits.

Events

There are many events and organizations that schedule activities of various kinds in the state of Alaska. Here are some of them.

Sports: Iditarod Trail Race (Anchorage), Great Alaska Shootout (Anchorage), North American Sled Dog Championships (Fairbanks), Solstice Game (Fairbanks), World Eskimo Indian Olympics (Fairbanks), Yukon Quest International Dog Sled Race (Fairbanks), Alcan 200 Snowmachine Rally (Haines), Golden North Salmon Derby (Juneau), Salmon Derby (Ketchikan), Bering Sea Ice Classic Golf Tournament (Nome), Seward Silver Salmon Derby (Seward), All Alaska Logging Championships (Sitka), Sitka Salmon Derby (Sitka), Tok Race of Champions (Tok), Halibut Derby (Valdez), Pink Salmon Derby (Valdez), Silver Salmon Derby (Valdez).

The starting line for the Iditarod Trail Race.

Arts and Crafts: The Crafts Fair at UAA (Anchorage), Festival of Native Arts (Fairbanks), Athapaskan Old-Time Fiddling Festival (Fairbanks), Summer Arts Festival (Fairbanks), Alaska Folk Festival (Juneau).

Music: Anchorage Opera (Anchorage), Quiana Alaska Native Dance Festival (Anchorage), Basically Bach Festival (Anchorage), Chilkat Indian Dances (Haines), Sitka Summer Music Festival (Sitka).

Entertainment: Fur Rendezvous (Anchorage), Iceworm Festival (Cordova), Fairbanks Ice Festival (Fairbanks), Golden Days (Fairbanks), North Pole Winter Carnival (Fairbanks), Oktoberfest (Fairbanks), Tanana Valley/Alaska State Fair (Fairbanks), Southeast Alaska State Fair (Haines), Taku Rondy at Eaglecrest (Juneau), Festival of the North (Ketchikan), Blueberry Festival (Ketchikan), King Crab Festival (Kodiak), Russian New Year and Masquerade Ball (Kodiak), Alaska State Fair (Palmer), Little Norway Festival (Petersburg), Alaska Day Celebration (Sitka), Progress Days (Soldotna), Bachelor Society Ball (Talkeetna), Gold Rush Days (Valdez), International Ice Climbing Festival (Valdez), Winter Carnival (Valdez), Tent City Winter Festival (Wrangell).

Tours: Matanuska River (Anchorage), 26 Glacier Cruise (Anchorage), Fort Yukon (Circle), Denali Dog Tours (Denali National Park and Preserve), Nenana River Float Trips (Denali National Park and Preserve), Tundra Wildlife Tours (Denali National Park and Preserve), Chilkat Bald Eagle Preserve Float Trips (Haines), Kenai Fjords Tours (Seward), White Pass & Yukon Route (Skagway).

Theater: Alaska Experience Theater (Anchorage), Chilkat Center for the Arts (Haines), "Lady Lou Revue" (Juneau), "Cry of the Wild Ram" (Kodiak), Skagway in the Days of '98 With "Soapy Smith" (Skagway).

Famous People

Several famous people were born in the state of Alaska. Here are two:

Benny Benson 1913-72, Chignik. Designed state flag at age 13

Scott Loucks b. 1956, Anchorage. Baseball player

Colleges and Universities

There are several colleges and universities in Alaska. Here are the more prominent, with their locations, dates of founding, and enrollments.

Alaska Pacific University, Anchorage, 1957, 809

University of Alaska, Anchorage, Anchorage, 1954, 12,860; *Fairbanks*, Fairbanks, 1917, 8,290; *Southeast*, Juneau, 1972, 2,787

Where To Get More Information

Alaska Division of Tourism
P.O. Box E-603
Juneau, AK 99811

Idaho

The state seal of Idaho, designed by Emma Edwards Green, was adopted in 1891. In the center of the seal there is a shield, with trees, mountains, farms, and a river representing Idaho's natural beauty. To the left, a woman holding a spear and scales signifies justice; to the right, a miner symbolizes Idaho's vast mineral resources. The state motto appears on a scroll above the shield, and beneath it an elk's head represents the state's wildlife. A sheaf of wheat, two cornucopias, and the state flower appear at the bottom; and a yellow border with "Great Seal of the State of Idaho" encircles the seal.

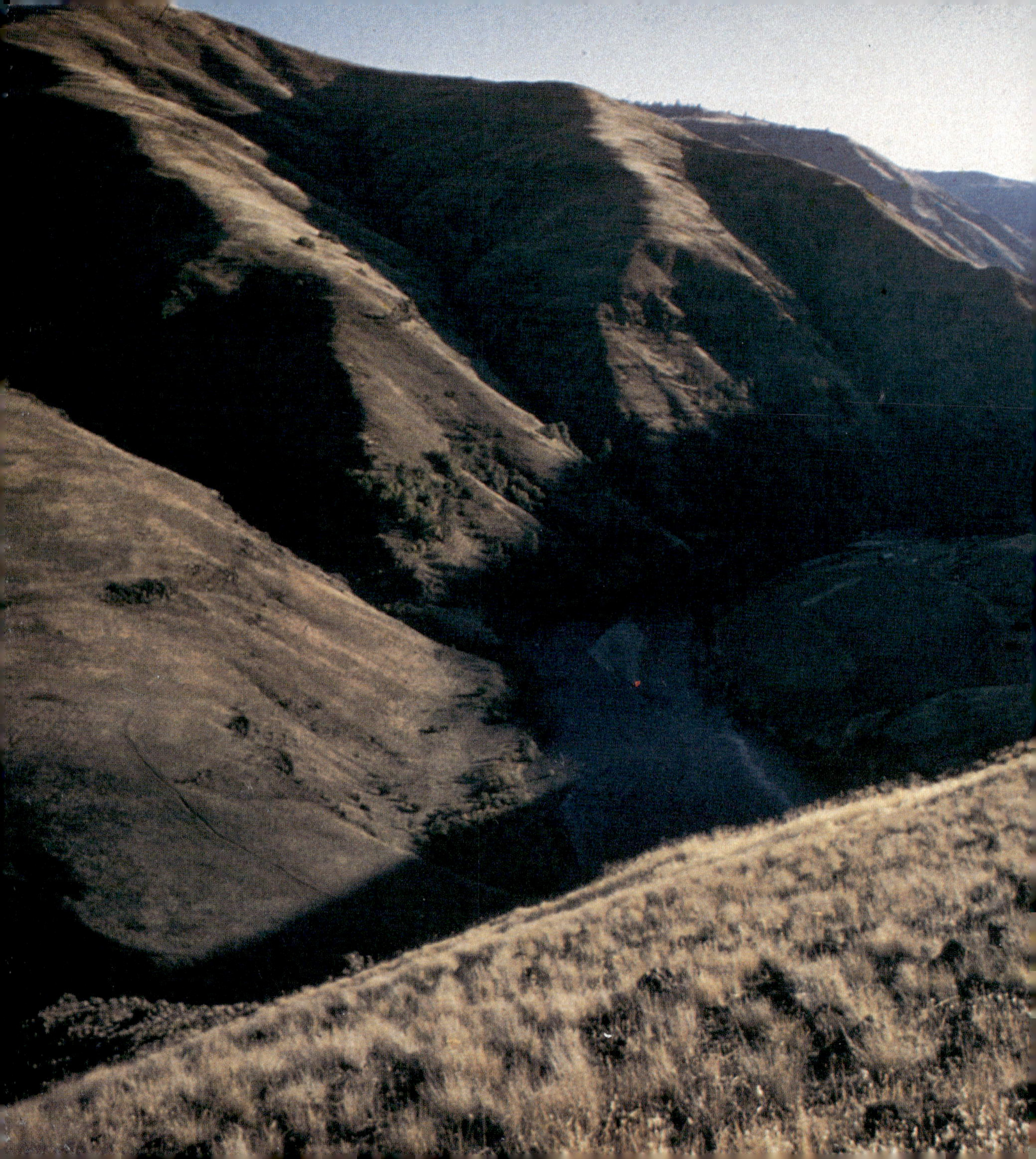

State Flag

The state flag, adopted in 1907, consists of the state seal on a blue field. A red band bordered in gold, with "State of Idaho" written upon it, appears beneath the seal. Gold fringe decorates the edges.

State Motto
Esto Perpetua

This Italian phrase, meaning "It is forever," is a quote from Pietro Sarpi, the Venetian theologian and mathematician.

The 12,000 acre Nez Perce National Historic Park provides visitors with a rich and varied look at both tribal culture and white exploration and settlements.

BRITISH COLUMBIA
ALBERTA
State Capital
Cities or towns
OF SPECIAL INTEREST
N
WASHINGTON
MONTANA
OREGON
IDAHO
WYOMING
NEVADA
UTAH
KANIKSU NATIONAL FOREST
Coeur d'Alene
COEUR D'ALENE NATIONAL FOREST
Kellogg
COEUR D'ALENE INDIAN RESERVATION
SAINT JOE NATIONAL FOREST
Moscow
CLEARWATER NATIONAL FOREST
Lewiston
Lewiston Orchards
NEZ PERCE NATIONAL FOREST
NEZ PERCE INDIAN RESERVATION
BITTERROOT NATIONAL FOREST
PAYETTE NATIONAL FOREST
SALMON NATIONAL FOREST
BOISE NATIONAL FOREST
SAWTOOTH NATIONAL FOREST
CHALLIS NATIONAL FOREST
TARGHEE NATIONAL FOREST
ST. ANTHONY
Caldwell
Boise
Nampa
Arco
CRATERS OF THE MOON NATIONAL MONUMENT
Idaho Falls
CARIBOU NATIONAL FOREST
FORT HALL INDIAN RESERVATION
Blackfoot
Mountain Home
Snake River
Alameda
Pocatello
Twin Falls
Burley
DUCK VALLEY INDIAN RESERVATION
SAWTOOTH NATIONAL FOREST
Montpelier
0 10 20 40 60 80 100 120 Miles
0 10 20 40 60 80 100 120 140 160 180 200 Kilometres

Idaho

State Capital

In 1863, when the Idaho Territory was formed, Lewiston was chosen as the capital. Boise became the capital the following year and has remained so ever since. Construction began on the capitol building in 1905, with the central part being completed in 1911, and the legislative wings ready for use by 1920. The cost of the structure, which is modeled after the U.S. Capitol, was almost $2.3 million. The exterior of the building is faced with Idaho sandstone, while the interior contains marble from Vermont, Alaska, Georgia, and Italy. On the top of the dome stands a bronze-coated, solid copper eagle. The eight columns surrounding the rotunda are made of scagliola, a material that resembles marble and that is composed of granite, marble dust, glue, and gypsum.

The Idaho State Capitol is built from local sandstone in the Classic Revival style and closely resembles the national Capitol in Washington, D.C.

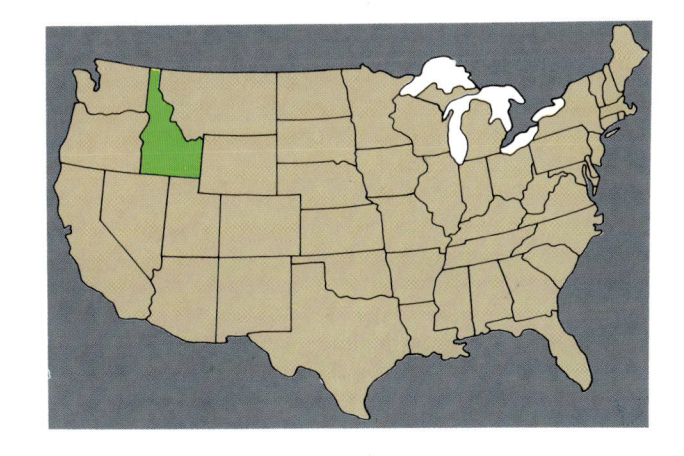

State Name and Nickname

The name Idaho was originally believed to be a Shoshone word meaning "gem of the mountains." In reality, it had been invented by George M. Willing as a name for the Colorado Territory. When Congress designated the Idaho Territory in 1863, the true origin of the word was still generally unknown.

Idaho is known popularly as the *Gem State,* or *Gem of the Mountains.*

State Flower

The state legislature selected Syringa, *Philadelphus lewisii,* as state flower in 1931.

State Tree

In 1935, the white pine, *Pinus monticola,* was designated state tree.

State Bird

In a vote by school children in 1931, the mountain bluebird, *Sialia currucoides,* was chosen state bird.

The state flower of Idaho is the Syringa.

State Gem

The star garnet was named state gem in 1967.

State Horse

The Appaloosa was adopted as state horse in 1975.

State Song

"Here We Have Idaho," with music by Sallie Hume Douglas and words by McKinley Helm and Albert J. Tompkins, was designated state song in 1931.

Population

The population of Idaho in 1990 was 1,011,986, making it the 42nd largest state. There are 12.1 people per square mile, 54 percent of the population live in towns and cities. About 98 percent of Idaho's people were born in the state, and approximately 10,400 Indians reside there.

Geography and Climate

Bounded on the north by the Canadian province of British Columbia, on the east by Montana and Wyoming, on the south by Utah and Nevada, and on the west by Oregon and Washington, Idaho has an area of 83,564 square miles, making it the 13th largest state. The climate is influenced by Pacific westerly winds. The mountain wilderness has cool summers and severe winters, while the populated valleys have a mild climate. It is drier and colder in the southeast. The Snake River plains are in the south; mountains, canyons, and gorges are in the central region; and the northern region is subalpine. The highest point in the state, at 12,662 feet, is Borah Peak in Custer County, and the lowest point, at 710 feet, is along the Clearwater and Snake rivers in Nez Percé County. The major waterways are the Bear, Clearwater, Payette, Salmon, and Snake rivers. Pend Oreille Lake is the largest in the state.

Industries

The principal industries of the state are agriculture, manufacturing, tourism, lumber, mining, and electronics. The chief manufactured products are processed foods, lumber and wood products, chemical products, primary metals, fabricated metal products, machinery, and electronic components.

Agriculture

The chief crops of the state are potatoes, peas, sugar beets, alfalfa seed, wheat, hops, barley, plums and prunes, mint, onions, corn, cherries, apples, and hay. Idaho is also a livestock state. There are estimated to be 1.62 million cattle, 80,000 hogs and pigs, 324,000 sheep, and 1.28 million chickens and turkeys on its farms. Yellow and white pine, Douglas fir, and white spruce are harvested. Phosphate rock, silver, gold, sand, and gravel are important mineral products.

Government

The governor of Idaho is elected to a four-year term, as are the lieutenant governor, secretary of state, auditor, treasurer, attorney general, and superintendent of public instruction. The state legislature, which meets annually, consists of a 42-member senate and an 84-member house of representatives. Each of the state's 33 legislative districts elects from one to three senators and from one to four representatives. Senators and representatives serve two-year terms. The most recent constitution was adopted in 1889, eleven months before Idaho became a state. In addition to its two United States senators, the state has two representatives in the U.S. House of Representatives. Idaho has four votes in the electoral college.

History

Artifacts found at campsites and markings on rocks indicate that 10,000 years ago Indians lived in what is now Idaho. Although the Nez Percé and the Shoshone were the largest tribes, the Coeur d'Alene, Pend d'Oreille, Kutenai, and Bannock also inhabited the region.

The first Europeans to

explore the area were Meriwether Lewis and William Clark, who sailed down the Snake and Clearwater rivers on their way to the Pacific in 1805. In 1809, David Thompson, a Canadian, established a fur trading post on Pend Oreille Lake. Fur trapping and trading were carried on in the region during the next three decades, with two additional trading posts—Fort Hall and Fort Boise—built in 1834. Two years later, Henry H. Spalding, a Presbyterian missionary, and his wife established the Lapwai Mission Station among the Nez Percé Indians. It wasn't until 1860, however, that a group of Mormons founded the first permanent settlement at Franklin.

During that same year, gold was discovered at Orofino Creek, and thousands of prospectors flocked to the area. In 1863, Congress established the Idaho Territory, which included all of Montana and most of Wyoming. The boundaries were finalized after the creation of the Montana Territory in 1864 and the Wyoming Territory in 1868. Idaho became the 43rd state in the Union in 1890.

Several confrontations with the Indians occurred in the late 1870s. The U.S. Army attempted to move the Nez Percé tribe from Oregon to the Lapwai Reservation in Idaho in 1877. The Indians, led by Chief Joseph, defeated the U.S. troops in a battle at White Bird Canyon in north-central Idaho on June 17. Soon after, however, they were forced to surrender, and agreed to return to the reservation. A year later, the Bannock Indians, in need of food and disturbed by the loss of their hunting grounds, clashed with U.S. troops. Their leader, Chief Buffalo Horn, was killed and they, too, surrendered.

Mining increased in importance after 1863. In the 1890s, disputes erupted between the mine owners and miners, and federal troops had to be called in to put an end to the violence. In 1899, Governor Frank Steunenberg declared martial law and again called in the troops.

Food shortages created by World War I brought prosperity for Idaho's farmers. It was short-lived, however, and during the

A dramatic view of Yellowstone National Park.

Idaho

1920s many farmers fell on hard times. Aided by federal projects such as the Civilian Conservation Corps, Idaho began to rebuild while the rest of the nation was suffering from the Great Depression of the 1930s.

World War II again created a demand for Idaho's farm products, and factories produced airplanes and arms for the war effort. Following the war, the lumber industry and manufacturing increased in importance. The National Reactor Testing Station was built near Idaho Falls, and nuclear energy was used to generate electricity for the first time in 1951.

Today, many small industries are moving into the state. While agriculture is still an essential part of Idaho's economy, tourism has become the third most important industry.

Sports

Many sporting events on the collegiate and secondary school levels are played throughout the state. In addition, hunting, fishing, and skiing are also popular pastimes.

Major Cities

Boise (population 102,160). The capital of Idaho, settled in 1862 during the gold rush days, is the state's largest city, as well as its business, financial, and transportation center. Its low cost of living and liberal tax laws have attracted many national and multinational firms, which maintain their headquarters here.

Things to see in Boise:
State Capitol, Julia Davis Park, Idaho State Historical Society Museum, Boise City Zoo, Boise Art Museum, Boise Interagency Fire Center, Discovery Center of Idaho, First United Methodist Church (1960), Idaho Botanical Garden, Table Rock, Howard Platt Gardens and Union Pacific Depot, St. Michael's Episcopal Cathedral (1900), Old Idaho Penitentiary (1870), World Center for Birds of Prey, Wild Waters Waterslide Theme Park, Eagle Island State Park, and Lucky Peak State Park.

Pocatello (population 46,340). Founded in 1882, this city is a major railroad junction between Omaha, Nebraska, and Portland, Oregon. Originally part of the Fort Hall Indian Reservation, it was named for the Bannock Indian chief who gave the Utah & Northern Railroad the right of way to build a Salt Lake City-to-Butte rail line.

Things to see in Pocatello:
Idaho Museum of Natural History, Bannock County Historical Museum, Ross Park, Old Fort Hall Replica, and Standrod House.

Places to Visit

The National Park Service maintains three areas in the state of Idaho: Craters of the Moon National Monument, Yellowstone National Park, and Nez Percé National Historical Park. In addition, there are 18 state recreation areas.

Arco: Experimental Breeder Reactor Number 1. Visitors may tour nuclear reactors and a reactor control room at the site of the first atomic reactor

to generate electricity.
Blackfoot: Bingham County Historical Museum. This restored 1905 homestead contains a gun collection, Indian relics, and antique furniture.
Buhl: Balanced Rock. This 40-foot-high tower of rock resembles a mushroom cloud from an atomic bomb.
Coeur d'Alene: Silverwood. This turn-of-the-century mining town theme park features an antique airplane museum, a wild animal exhibit, and rides.
Kellogg: Old Mission State Park. This park contains the Coeur d'Alene Mission of the Sacred Heart, a restored Indian mission and the oldest building in the state.
Lewiston: Castle Museum. This three-story house, built in 1906 of handmade cement blocks, was modeled after a Scottish castle.
Montpelier: Minnetonka Cave. The cave, which lies at 7,700 feet above sea level, contains fossils of plants and marine animals from a prehistoric sea.
Moscow: Appaloosa Horse Museum. This museum features exhibits and artifacts relating to the Appaloosa horse, as well as cowboy and Nez Percé Indian memorabilia.
Rexburg: Teton Flood Museum. This museum contains displays relating to the break in the Teton Dam that resulted in the 1976 flood.
Salmon: Lemhi. This historic ghost town, named for a character in *The Book of Mormon*, was built in 1855.
Sandpoint: Vintage Wheel Museum. The antique car collection housed at this museum includes a Stanley Steamer and a 1913 Cadillac.
Shoshone: Shoshone Indian Ice Caves. These caves, which maintain a constant temperature of 30-33 degrees Fahrenheit, contain beautiful ice formations.
Wallace: Northern Pacific Depot Railroad Museum. The first floor of this restored station contains a re-creation of an early 1900s railroad depot, as well as railroad memorabilia.
Weiser: Fiddlers Hall of Fame. This museum features a collection of old time fiddles.

Events

There are many events and organizations that schedule activities of various kinds in the state of Idaho. Here are some of them.

Sports: Horse racing at Les Bois Park (Boise), River Super Float (Boise), Burley Speedboat Regatta (Burley), Little Britches Rodeo (Caldwell), War Bonnet Roundup (Idaho Falls), horse racing at the Jerome County Fairgrounds (Jerome), Chariot Races (Jerome), NAIA World Series Baseball Tournament (Lewiston), Regional Hydroplane Races (Lewiston), Jet Boat Race (Lewiston), Snake River Stampede (Nampa), Frontier Rodeo (Pocatello), Pacific Northwest Sled Dog Championship Races (Priest Lake), International Draft Horse Show and Sale (Sandpoint), Sandpoint Winter Carnival (Sandpoint), Duchin Celebrity Invitational Cup (Sun Valley), Western Days (Twin Falls).

Arts and Crafts: Art on the Green (Coeur d'Alene), Gem Dandy Days (Jerome), Arts in the Park (Shoshone), Sun Valley Center Arts and Crafts Fair (Sun Valley).

Music: American Festival Ballet (Boise), Boise Philharmonic (Boise), Jazzfest (Coeur d'Alene), Music Festival (McCall), Lionel Hampton/Chevron Jazz Festival (Moscow), Summer Band Concert Series (Pocatello), Idaho International Folk Dance Festival (Rexburg), Old Time Fiddlers' Jamboree (Shoshone), Sun Valley Music Festival (Sun Valley),

Idaho

National Oldtime Fiddlers' Contest (Weiser).

Entertainment: Massacre Rocks Rendezvous (American Falls), Eastern Idaho State Fair (Blackfoot), Old Boise Days (Boise), Western Idaho State Fair (Boise), Harvestfest (Buhl), Sagebrush Days (Buhl), Cassia County Fair and Rodeo (Burley), Canyon County Fair (Caldwell), Oktoberfest (Coeur d'Alene), North Idaho Fair (Coeur d'Alene), Shoshone-Bannock Indian Festival (Fort Hall), Winter Festival (Grangeville), Jerome County Fair (Jerome), Septemberfest (Kellogg), Rendezvous-Pioneer Days Celebration (Lava Hot Springs), Dogwood Festival (Lewiston), Lewiston Air Fair (Lewiston), Lewiston Roundup (Lewiston), Nez Percé County Fair (Lewiston), Winter Carnival (McCall), Bear Lake County Fair and Rodeo (Montpelier), Moscow Mardi Gras and Beaux Arts Ball (Moscow), Latah County Fair (Moscow), Rendezvous in the Park (Moscow), Clearwater County Fair and Lumberjack Days (Orofino), Minidoka County Fair and Rodeo (Rupert), Fremont County Pioneer Days (St. Anthony), Paul Bunyan Days (St. Maries), Salmon River Day (Salmon), Festival at Sandpoint (Sandpoint), Lincoln County Fair (Shoshone), Wagon Days (Sun Valley), Twin Falls County Fair and Rodeo (Twin Falls).

Tours: Boise Tour Train (Boise), Hells Canyon Excursions (Lewiston), Barker-Ewing River Trips (Salmon), Sierra Silver Mine Tour (Wallace), jet boat tours (Weiser).

Theater: Morrison Center for the Performing Arts (Boise), Idaho Shakespeare Festival (Boise), Idaho Repertory Theater (Moscow).

Famous People

Many famous people were born in the state of Idaho. Here are a few:

Ezra Taft Benson b. 1899, Whitney. Secretary of Agriculture and president of the Church of Jesus Christ of Latter-Day Saints

Gutzon Borglum 1867-1941, near Bear Lake. Sculptor: Mount Rushmore National Monument

The Wagon Days Parade, held over the Labor Day weekend in Ketchum, Idaho, is the largest non-motorized parade in the west. The parade originated in the 1950s, in celebration of Ketchum's mining heritage.

Frank Church 1924-84, Boise. Senate leader

Ken Dayley b. 1959, Jerome. Baseball pitcher

Larry Jackson 1931-90, Nampa. Baseball pitcher

William M. Jardine 1879-1955, Oneida County. Secretary of Agriculture

Kamaiakan 1800-80, near Lewiston. Indian leader

Harmon Killebrew b. 1936, Payette. Hall of Fame baseball player

Vance Law b. 1956, Boise. Baseball player

Vern Law b. 1930, Meridian. Baseball pitcher

Ezra Pound 1885-1972, Hailey. Poet and critic: *Homage to Sextus Propertius, Hugh Selwyn Mauberley*

James Rainwater 1917-86, Council. Nobel Prize-winning physicist

Sacagawea 1787-1812, ?. Shoshone interpreter

Lana Turner b. 1920, Wallace. Film actress: *The Postman Always Rings Twice, Peyton Place*

Herman Welker 1906-57, Cambridge. Senate leader

Larry Wilson b. 1938, Rigby. Football player

Colleges and Universities

There are several colleges and universities in Idaho. Here are the more prominent, with their locations, dates of founding, and enrollments.

Boise State University, Boise, 1932, 12,000

College of Idaho, Caldwell, 1891, 1,189

Idaho State University, Pocatello, 1901, 8,700

Lewis-Clark State College, Lewiston, 1955, 2,164

Northwest Nazarene College, Nampa, 1913, 1,133

University of Idaho, Moscow, 1889, 9,967

Where To Get More Information

Idaho Travel Council
700 W. State St., 2nd floor
Boise, ID 83720
1-800-635-7820

Oregon

The state seal of Oregon, adopted in 1903, contains a shield partially encircled by 33 stars and topped by the American Eagle. Pictured on the shield are mountains, forests, an elk, a covered wagon with a team of oxen, the sun setting over the Pacific Ocean, a departing British warship, and an arriving American merchant ship. The last two represent the end of British rule and the rise of American power. A ribbon inscribed with "The Union" divides the shield; and a sheaf of wheat, a plow, and a pickax below the ribbon symbolize agriculture and mining. The border around the seal reads "State of Oregon" and "1859"—the year of the state's admission to the Union.

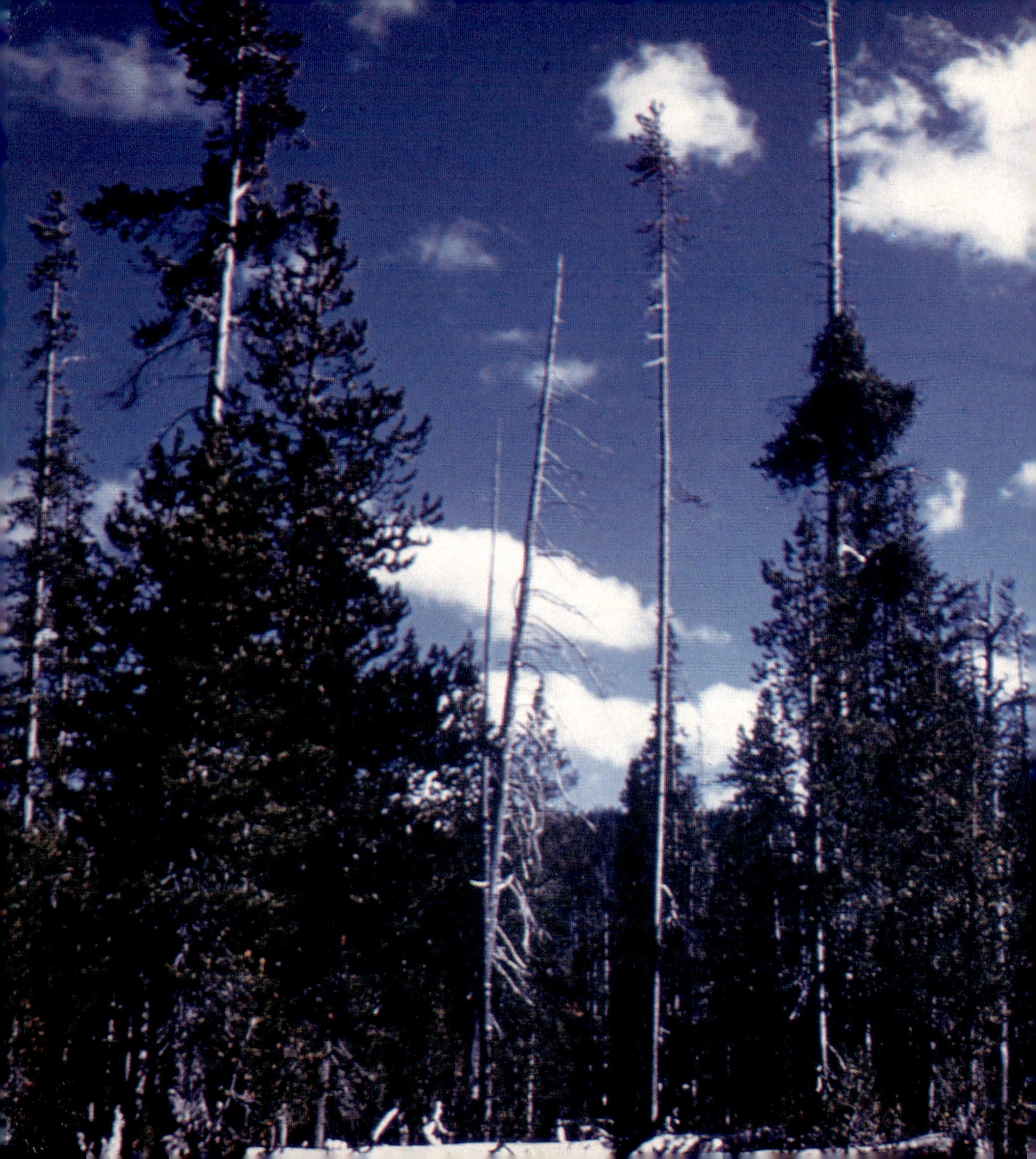

State Flag

The state flag of Oregon consists of the shield and stars from the state seal printed in gold on a navy blue background. "State of Oregon" appears above the shield and "1859" is inscribed below it. The reverse side contains a picture of a beaver, Oregon's state animal. The flag is sometimes trimmed with gold fringe.

State Motto

She Flies with Her Own Wings

This motto, adopted in 1987, was originally printed on the territorial seal in Latin. It replaces *The Union*, which had been designated in 1957.

Crater Lake, created by an eruption of Mount Mazama, was made a national park in 1902.

WASHINGTON
State Capital
Cities or towns
OF SPECIAL INTEREST
Astoria
Saint Helens
Forest Grove
Portland
Gresham
The Dalles
SIUSLAW NATIONAL FOREST
MOUNT HOOD NATIONAL FOREST
Dallas
Salem
WARM SPRINGS INDIAN RESERVATION
Newport
Corvallis
PACIFIC OCEAN
Brownsville
SIUSLAW NATIONAL FOREST
WILLAMETTE NATIONAL FOREST
Eugene
Bend
Cottage Grove
DESCHUTES NATIONAL FOREST
North Bend
Coos Bay
UMPQUA NATIONAL FOREST
WINEMA NATIONAL FOREST
Barnes
Roseburg
Bandon
CRATER LAKE NATIONAL PARK
N
ROGUE RIVER NATIONAL FOREST
SISKIYOU NATIONAL FOREST
Grants Pass
Medford
FREMONT NATIONAL FOREST
Klamath Falls
OREGON CAVES NATIONAL MONUMENT
Ashland
Altamont
FREMONT NATIONAL FOREST
CALIFORNIA
0 10 20 40 60 80 100 120 Miles
0 10 20 40 60 80 100 120 140 160 180 200 Kilometres

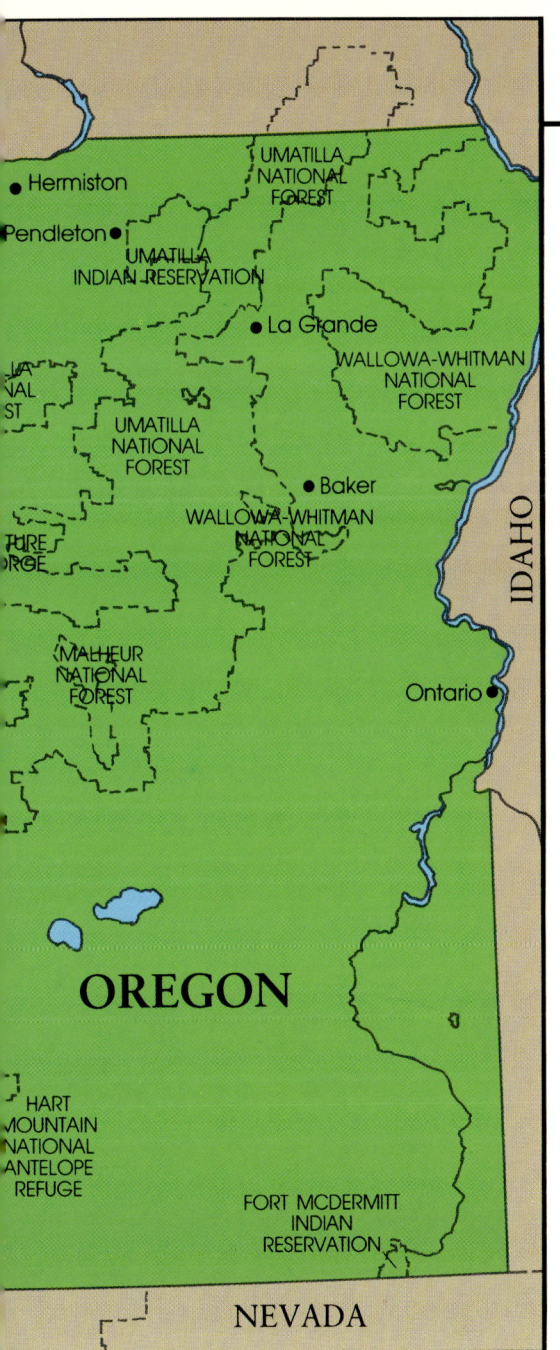

The Oregon State Capitol is a relatively new edifice, built in a modern style.

State Capital

Salem has been the capital of Oregon since 1855, four years before statehood. The present capitol building, constructed between 1935 and 1939, is the third structure to house the state's government. Two previous capitols, built in 1854 and 1872, were destroyed by fire. The four-story Greek-style building, designed by Francis Keally, is constructed of white Vermont marble and bronze and cost about $2,500,000. A bronze statue, enameled in gold leaf, stands on top of the cylindrical tower. *Pioneer*, by sculptor Ulric H. Ellerhusen, is a tribute to the state's early settlers. Wings were added to the building in 1977 at a cost of $12,025,303.

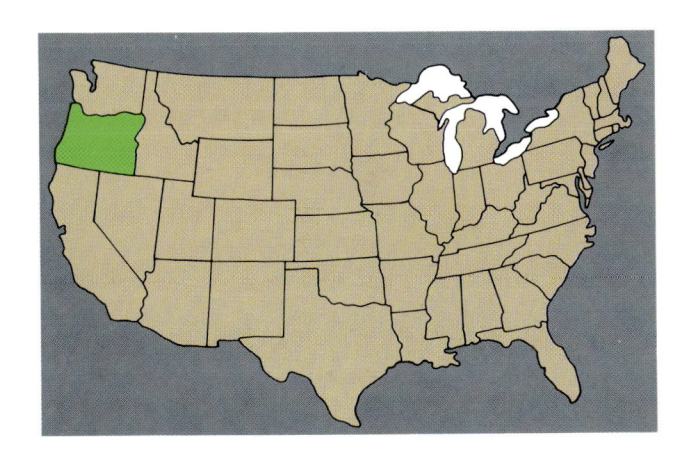

State Name and Nicknames

There are several theories concerning the origin of the name Oregon. French Canadians used the word *ouragon*, meaning "storm" or "hurricane," in connection with the Columbia River, which they often called "the river of storms." The name may have been derived from either of two Spanish words—*orejon*, meaning "big ear," used in reference to the tribes of the region, or *oregano*, because of the abundance of wild sage growing in the area.

Officially, Oregon is known as the *Beaver State* because of the importance of fur trapping in the state's history. The state has also been referred to as the *Web-foot State* for its abundant rainfall, and the *Hard-case State* for the many hardships encountered by the early settlers.

State Flower

The Oregon grape, *Berberis aquifolium*, was selected by the state legislature as state flower in 1899.

State Tree

The Douglas fir, *Pseudotsuga menziessii*, was chosen state tree in 1939.

State Bird

In 1927, the western meadowlark, *Sturnella neglecta*, was proclaimed state bird by the governor after a vote by the state's school children.

State Animal

The American Beaver, *Castor canadensis*, was designated state animal in 1969.

The Oregon grape is the state flower.

The Oregon state bird is the meadowlark.

State Dance

The square dance was chosen by the state legislature as official state dance in 1977.

State Fish

The Chinook salmon, *Oncorhynchus tshawytscha*, was selected as state fish in 1961.

State Gemstone

The Oregon sunstone, a large, brightly colored, transparent gem, was declared official state gemstone by the 1987 legislature.

State Hostess

In 1969, Miss Oregon was named state hostess.

Oregon

State Insect
The Oregon Swallowtail butterfly, *Papilio oregonius*, was adopted as state insect in 1979.

State Rock
In 1965, the thunderegg, or geode, was chosen state rock.

State Song
"Oregon, My Oregon," with words by J. A. Buchanan and music by Henry B. Murtagh, was designated state song in 1927.

Population
The population of Oregon in 1990 was 2,853,733, making it the 30th most populous state. There are 29.4 people per square mile—67.9 percent of the population live in towns and cities. About 96 percent of the people were born in the United States.

Geography and Climate
Bounded on the north by Washington, on the east by Idaho, on the south by Nevada and California, and on the west by the Pacific Ocean, Oregon has an area of 97,073 square miles, making it the tenth largest state. The climate is varied, with mild temperatures and high humidity in the coastal areas, and continental dryness and extreme temperatures in the interior. The main land areas include the Coast Range of rugged mountains bordering the Pacific Ocean, the fertile Willamette River Valley to the east, the Cascade Mountain Range of volcanic peaks to the east of the valley, the Columbia Plateau to the east of the Cascades, the Basin and Range region to the south of the plateau, and the Klamath Mountains in the southwest corner of the state. The highest point, at 11,239 feet, is Mount Hood in Clackamas and Hood River counties, and the lowest point is at sea level along the Pacific Ocean. The major waterways of the state are the Columbia, Willamette, Snake, Deschutes, and John Day rivers. Crater Lake in the Cascade Mountains, at 1,932 feet, is the deepest lake in the United States.

Industries
The principal industries of Oregon are forestry, agriculture, manufacturing, tourism, printing and publishing, and high technology. The chief manufactured goods are lumber and wood products, foods, machinery, fabricated metals, paper, and primary metals.

Agriculture
The chief crops of the state are hay, grass seed, farm forest products, wheat, potatoes, onions, and pears. Oregon is also a livestock state. There are estimated to be 1.4 million cattle, 100,000 hogs and pigs, 475,000 sheep, and 21.9 million chickens and turkeys on its farms. Douglas fir, hemlock, and ponderosa pine are harvested. Crushed stone and construction sand and gravel are important

mineral products. Commercial fishing brings in $78.9 million per year.

Government

The governor is elected to a four-year term, as are the attorney general, labor commissioner, secretary of state, superintendent of public instruction, and treasurer. The state legislature, which meets in odd-numbered years, consists of a 30-member senate and a 60-member house of representatives. Each of the 30 senatorial districts elects one senator to a four-year term, and each of the 60 representative districts elects one representative to a two-year term. The most recent constitution was adopted in 1857, two years prior to statehood. In addition to its two United States senators, Oregon has five representatives in the U.S. House of Representatives. The state has seven votes in the electoral college.

History

Oregon was home to many Indian tribes prior to the arrival of the Europeans. The Chinook, Clackama, Multnomah, and Tillamook tribes lived in the northwest; the Bannock, Cayuse, Paiute, Umatilla, and Nez Percé occupied the area east of the Cascade Mountains; and the Klamath and Modoc inhabited the south.

Spanish sailors traveling from Mexico to the Philippines during the 1500s and 1600s were the first to see the coast of Oregon. English expeditions were led by explorer Sir Francis Drake in 1579 and by British naval officer Captain James Cook in 1778. In 1792, American explorer Robert Gray sailed into the mouth of a great river, which he named Columbia, after his ship. During that same year,

The Historic Bush House in Salem, Oregon, was built by Asahel Bush II, the founder of the Oregon Statesman and the Ladd and Bush Bank.

Oregon

George Vancouver of Great Britain explored and mapped the coast. In 1805, Meriwether Lewis and William Clark, traveling overland, arrived at the mouth of the Columbia, thus strengthening the claim of the United States to the region.

During the early 1800s, Russia, Spain, Great Britain, and the United States all claimed parts of Oregon, which stretched from Alaska to California, and from the Pacific to the Rocky Mountains. The southern border of Oregon was agreed upon in a treaty between the United States and Spain in 1819. Because Great Britain and the United States were unable to decide on a boundary line separating their claims, citizens of both countries were allowed to settle in the region. Russia's claims to the area were relinquished in treaties with Great Britain in 1824 and the United States in 1825.

The white settlement of Oregon began in 1811, when John Jacob Astor founded a fur-trading post at Astoria. John McLoughlin, who became known as the "Father of Oregon," ruled the Oregon region for about 20 years as head of the Hudson's Bay Company, a British trading firm based at Fort Vancouver. The first permanent American settlement was established in 1834 by Methodist missionaries near present-day Salem in the Willamette Valley.

The first large arrival of American settlers into the area, which began in 1843, increased the need to resolve the boundary dispute with Great Britain. In his presidential campaign slogan of 1844—"Fifty-Four Forty or Fight"—James K. Polk emphasized the U.S. claim to land south of latitude 54 degrees, 40 minutes. The Oregon boundary was finally fixed at the 49th parallel when President Polk signed a treaty with Great Britain in 1846. Oregon became a territory two years later, and its present boundaries were fixed in 1853. On February 14, 1859, Oregon became the 33rd state in the Union.

Between 1847 and 1878, the Oregon Territory was the site of several Indian wars. After the Civil War, Oregon's population increased quickly despite the Indian attacks, which continued for the next 15 years. By 1890, there were 300,000 people living in the state.

In 1902, the state legislature passed laws giving voters more direct control over the government. The *initiative* and *referendum*, procedures allowing voters to take part in lawmaking, and the *recall*, a procedure for removing officials from office, became known as the Oregon System. Women were given the right to vote in 1912.

Although Oregon suffered during the Great Depression of the 1930s, it was not hit as hard as the more industrialized states. The federal government financed the construction of the

Rick Adelman guided the Portland Trail Blazers to the NBA Finals during the 1989-90 season, his first full season as head coach.

Bonneville Dam on the Columbia River. The project, which was completed in 1937, provided a new source of electricity for industry. Metal shipbuilding thrived during World War II, and Portland became important for shipping supplies to Russia and the U.S. military stationed in the Pacific. Following the war, new dams built on the Columbia River increased the state's supply of inexpensive electric power, thus contributing to Oregon's industrial growth.

Today, Oregon is the nation's leader in lumber production. Its industry is still growing, and agriculture continues to be an important part of the state's economy.

Sports

Many sporting events on the collegiate and secondary school levels are played throughout the state. In football, the University of

Oregon

Oregon won the Rose Bowl in 1917, and Oregon State University won in 1942. The University of Oregon also won the first N.C.A.A. basketball tournament in 1939.

On the professional level, the Portland Trail Blazers of the National Basketball Association play their home games in Memorial Coliseum.

Major Cities

Portland (population 418,470). Founded in 1845, Portland was named by Francis Pettygrove after his hometown in Maine. The pioneer town grew steadily, and by the turn of the century had become a thriving metropolis. Located on the banks of the Willamette River, Oregon's largest city is a busy port, visited by more than 1,400 ships each year.

Things to see in Portland: American Advertising Museum, Audubon Society of Portland, Children's Museum, Crystal Springs Rhododendron Gardens, The Grotto, Hoyt Arboretum, Ira Keller Fountain, James F. Bybee House (1858), John Palmer House, Leach Botanical Park, Maveety Gallery, Old Church, Oregon Art Institute, Oregon Historical Society, Oregon Maritime Center and Museum, Oregon Museum of Science and Industry, Peninsula Rose Garden, Pittock Mansion (1914), Portland Police Historical Museum, Washington Park, Washington Park Zoo, and World Forestry Center.

Salem (population 89,233). Oregon's capital was settled in 1840 by missionary Jason Lee, who tried to teach the Indians farming as well as religion. Eventually, Lee founded the Oregon Institute, which became the present-day Willamette University. Today, the state government, food processing, and light manufacturing form the basis of Salem's economy.

Things to see in Salem: Bush's Pasture Park, Bush Barn Art Center, Bush Conservatory, Bush House Museum, Deepwood Estate, Enchanted Forest, Mission Mill Village, Jason Lee House, Parsonage, John D. Boon Home, Thomas Kay Woolen Mill (1889), Silver Falls State Park, and the State Capitol.

Places to Visit

The National Park Service maintains five areas in the state of Oregon: Crater Lake National Park, John Day Fossil Beds National Monument, Oregon Caves National Monument, McLoughlin House National Historic Site, and Fort Clatsop National Memorial. In addition, there are 90 state recreation areas.

Astoria: Columbia River Maritime Museum. This museum features exhibits relating to the history of the Columbia River and the northwest.

Bandon: West Coast Game Park. One of the west coast's largest animal petting parks features more than 450 animals on 21 acres.

Bend: High Desert Museum. Indoor/outdoor exhibits feature live animals, plants, and historical artifacts of the northwest desert region.

Brownsville: Living Rock Studios. In addition to oil paintings and a mineral

A 15-inch Brazilian Bahian doll, one of the beautiful collection at the Dolly Wares Museum.

collection, the studios also contain Biblical scenes portrayed in rock and wood carvings.

Cottage Grove: Cottage Grove Historical Museum. The museum is housed in an octagonal structure which was built in 1897 as a Catholic church.

Eugene: Willamette Science and Technology Center. Hands-on exhibits explore physics, biology, and computer science.

Florence: Dolly Wares Doll Museum. This museum houses a collection of more than 2,500 dolls from around the world.

Gold Hill: The Oregon Vortex. Strange magnetic forces cause mysterious effects, such as preventing visitors from standing erect.

John Day: Kam Wah Chung & Co. Museum. Originally built in the 1860s as a doctor's office, this museum includes a collection of more than 1,000 herbs and medicines used by an herbal doctor.

Lakeview: Hart Mountain National Antelope Refuge. This 275,000-acre refuge is home to pronghorn antelope, bighorn sheep, and golden eagles, as well as numerous other wildlife species.

Newberg: Hoover-Minthorn House Museum. Built in 1881, this memorial museum contains mementoes of the five years that Herbert Hoover spent here during his childhood.

Newport: Undersea Gardens. Large underwater windows provide visitors with views of marine animals and plants in their natural setting.

Port Orford: Prehistoric Gardens. Visitors can view life-size replicas of dinosaurs in a rain forest setting.

Redmond: Petersen's Rock Gardens. Replicas of famous structures are fashioned out of rock and petrified wood in a colorful setting.

Roseburg: Wildlife Safari. In addition to a drive-through park, this attraction features a petting zoo, animal shows, and elephant rides.

Seal Rock: Sea Gulch. Among the features to be found in this western theme park are over 400 chainsaw-sculpted human and animal figures.

The Dalles: Wonder Works Children's Museum. This museum features many hands-on exhibits, including a child-size space shuttle.

Tillamook: Pioneer Museum. This museum contains exhibits on various aspects of pioneer and Indian life.

Events

There are many events and organizations that schedule activities of various kinds in the state of Oregon. Here are some of them.

Sports: Rodeo and Race Meet (Burns), Columbia River Gorge Sailpark (Hood River), Cross Channel Swim (Hood River), Jordan Valley Rodeo (Jordan Valley), Chief Joseph Days Rodeo (Joseph), auto racing at Portland International Raceway

Oregon

(Portland), auto racing at Portland Speedway (Portland), Cascade Run-Off (Portland), greyhound racing at Multnomah Kennel Club (Portland), horseracing at Portland Meadows (Portland), Hot Air Balloon Classic (Portland), Indy Car World Series Race (Portland), Portland Marathon (Portland).

Arts and Crafts: Scandinavian Midsummer Festival (Astoria), Artquake Festival (Portland), Central Oregon Art Festival (Prineville), Salem Art Fair and Festival (Salem), East Linn Museum Quilt Show (Sweet Home), Arts and Crafts Fair (Yachats).

Music: The Oregon Coast

Artists of all ages display their talent at the Salem Art Fair.

Music Festival (Coos Bay), Bach Festival (Eugene), All-Northwest Barber Shop Ballad Contest and Gay Nineties Festival (Forest Grove), Bluegrass Festival (Hillsboro), Oregon Symphony Orchestra (Portland), Portland Opera Association (Portland), Rose City Blues Festival (Portland).

Entertainment: World Championship Timber Carnival (Albany), Winter Food (Ashland), Great Astoria Crab Feed and Seafood Festival (Astoria), Cranberry Festival (Bandon), Azalea Festival (Brookings), Beachcombers' Festival (Brookings), Pioneer Picnic (Brownsville), Harney County Fair (Burns), High Desert Hot Air Balloon Rally and Fiddle Contest (Burns), Obsidian Days (Burns), Waterfowl Festival (Burns), Sandcastle Contest (Cannon Beach), "62" Day Celebration (Canyon City), Sternwheeler Days (Cascade Locks), Da Vinci Days (Corvallis), Fleet of Flowers (Depoe Bay), Historic Preservation Week (Eugene), Rhododendron Festival (Florence), Peter Britt Festivals (Jacksonville), Kam Wah Chung Days (John Day), Oregon Trail Days (La Grande), Union County Fair (La Grande), Lake County Fair and Round-Up (Lakeview), Lebanon Strawberry Festival (Lebanon), Jefferson County Fair and Rodeo (Madras), Turkey-Rama (McMinnville), Pear Blossom Festival (Medford), Old-Fashioned Festival (Newberg), Loyalty Days and Sea Fair Festival (Newport), Japanese Obon Festival (Ontario), Malheur County Fair (Ontario), Ontario Winter Wonderland Parade (Ontario), Pendleton Round-Up (Pendleton), Frolic and Rodeo Festival (Philomath), Mount Hood Festival (Portland), Multnomah County Fair (Portland), Neighborfair (Portland), Pacific International Livestock Show (Portland), Portland Oktoberfest (Portland), Rose Festival (Portland), A Taste of Portland (Portland), "Wintering-In" (Portland), Rockhound Pow Wow (Prineville), Oregon State Fair (Salem), West Salem Waterfront Festival (Salem), Broiler Festival (Springfield), Christmas Parade (Springfield), Smelt Fry (Yachats).

Tours: Crater Lake Boat Tour (Crater Lake National Park), Snake River Boat Trips (Hells Canyon National Recreation Area), Oregon Caves tour (Oregon Caves National Monument), Victorian Home Tours (The Dalles).

Theater: Oregon Shakespeare Festival (Ashland), Linfield Little Theater (McMinnville), Dolores Winningstad Theater (Portland), Intermediate Theater (Portland), Portland Center for the Performing Arts (Portland), Willamette Center (Portland).

Famous People
Many famous people were born in the state of Oregon. Here are a few:

Danny Ainge b. 1959, Eugene. Basketball player

Wally Backman b. 1959, Hillsboro. Baseball player

Daniel Barbey 1889-1969, Portland. U.S. naval officer

Blanche Bates 1873-1941, Portland. Stage actress

James Beard 1903-85, Portland. Cookbook author

Beverly Cleary b. 1916, McMinnville. Children's book author

Dean Cromwell 1879-1962, Turner. Track-and-field coach

Homer Davenport 1867-1912, Silverton. Cartoonist

Margaret Osborne duPont b. 1918, Joseph. Tennis

Oregon

champion
Herbert Gaston 1881-1956, Halsey. Journalist and government official
Alfred C. Gilbert 1884-1961, Salem. Business leader and toy manufacturer
Neil Goldschmidt b. 1940, Eugene. Secretary of Transportation
Morris Graves b. 1910, Fox Valley. Artist
Mark Hatfield b. 1922, Dallas. Senate leader
Willis Hawley 1864-1941, near Monroe. Educator and congressman
Margaux Hemingway b. 1955, Portland. Film actress: *Lipstick*
Howard Hesseman b. 1940, Lebanon. Television and film actor: *WKRP in Cincinnati*, *Head of the Class*
Larry Jansen b. 1920, Verboort. Baseball pitcher
Joseph 1840-1904, Wallowa Valley. Indian leader
Dave Kingman b. 1948, Pendleton. Baseball player
Kenneth Latourette 1884-1968, Oregon City. Theologian
Mickey Lolich b. 1940, Portland. Baseball pitcher
Ranald MacDonald 1824-94, Fort George. Adventurer
Larry Mahan b. 1957, White Pass. Champion rodeo performer
Edwin Markham 1852-1940, Oregon City. Poet
Ross McIntire 1889-1959, Salem. Physician

Jane Powell began her show business career as a child, singing on the radio.

Douglas McKay 1893-1959, Portland. Secretary of the Interior
Dale Murphy b. 1956, Portland. Baseball player
Brent Musburger b. 1939, Portland. Broadcaster
Richard Neuberger 1912-60, Portland. Senate leader and journalist
Bob Packwood b. 1932, Portland. Senate leader
Linus Pauling b. 1901, Portland. Two-time Nobel Prize-winning chemist
River Phoenix b. 1970, Madras. Film actor: *Stand by Me*
Jane Powell b. 1929, Portland. Film actress: *Seven Brides for Seven Brothers*, *Deep in My Heart*
Ahmad Rashad b. 1949, Portland. Football player and broadcaster
Johnnie Ray 1927-90, Rosebud. Pop singer
John Reed 1887-1920, Portland. Journalist and political radical
Harold Reynolds b. 1960,

Eugene. Baseball player
Susan Ruttan b. 1950, Oregon City. Television actress: *L.A. Law*
Patricia Schroeder b. 1940, Portland. Congresswoman
Doc Severinsen b. 1927, Arlington. Bandleader and trumpeter
Paul Simon b. 1928, Eugene. Senate leader
Sally Struthers b. 1948, Portland. Television actress: *All in the Family, Gloria*

Colleges and Universities

There are many colleges and universities in Oregon. Here are the more prominent, with their locations, dates of founding, and enrollments.

Eastern Oregon State College, La Grande, 1929, 1,812
George Fox College, Newberg, 1891, 944
Lewis and Clark College, Portland, 1867, 2,721
Linfield College, McMinnville, 1849, 1,312
Marylhurst College for Lifelong Learning, Marylhurst, 1893, 1,031
Oregon Health Sciences University, Portland, 1974, 1,317
Oregon Institute of Technology, Klamath Falls, 1947, 3,023
Oregon State University, Corvallis, 1868, 15,958
Pacific University, Forest Grove, 1849, 1,398
Portland State University, Portland, 1946, 14,838
Reed College, Portland, 1904, 1,286
Southern Oregon State College, Ashland, 1926, 4,801
University of Oregon, Eugene, 1872, 17,818
University of Portland, Portland, 1901, 2,415
Western Oregon State College, Monmouth, 1856, 3,856
Willamette University, Salem, 1842, 2,223

Where To Get More Information
Tourism Division
Oregon Dept of Economic Development
775 Summer St. NE
Salem, OR 97310
1-800-543-8838 (in Oregon)
1-800-547-7842 (outside Oregon)

Washington

On the seal of the state of Washington is a picture of George Washington, along with the date 1889—the year of the state's admission to the Union. "The Seal of the State of Washington" is printed in the outer circle.

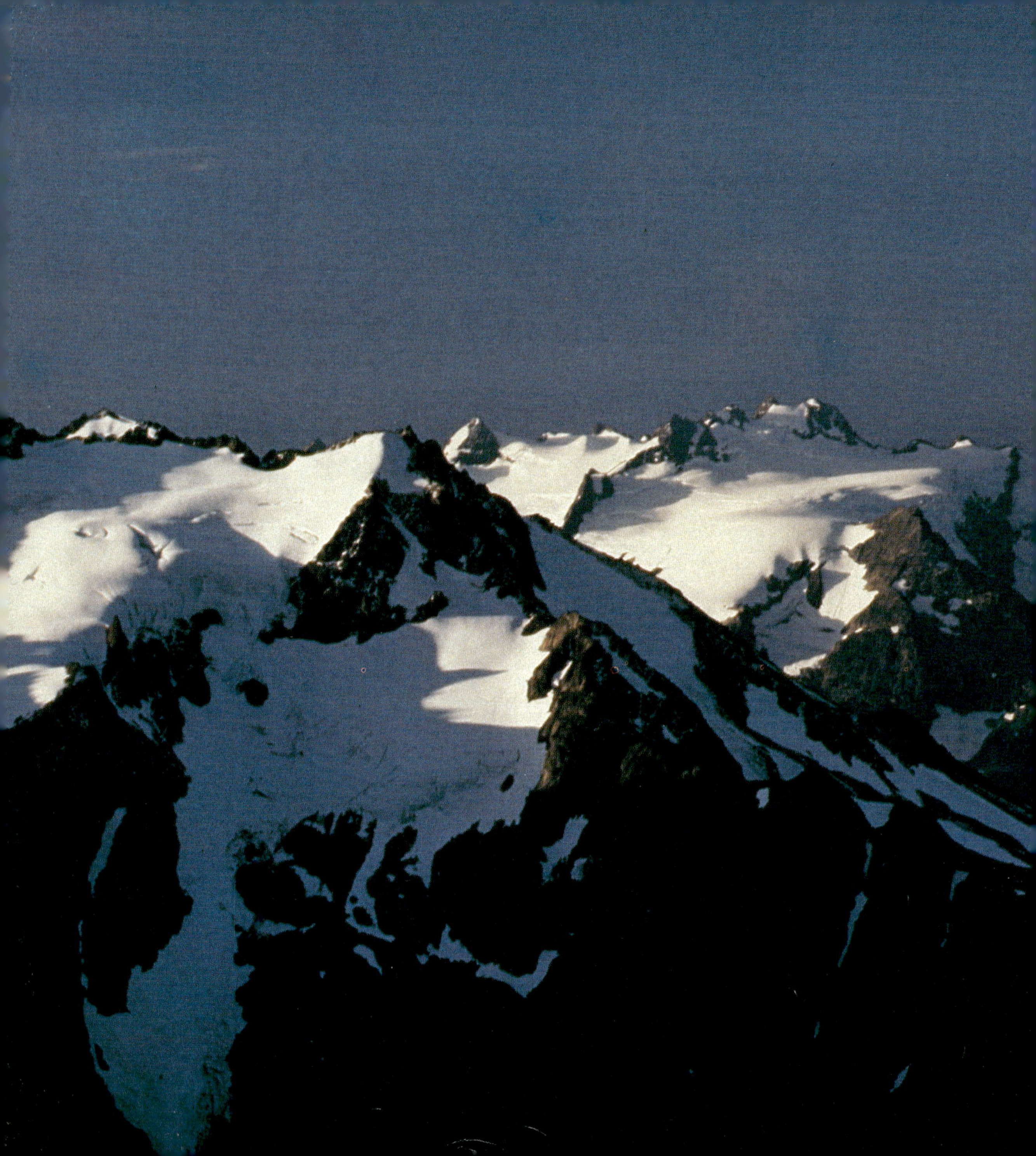

State Flag

The state flag of Washington was adopted in 1923 and changed slightly in 1925. The dark green field, which sometimes is fringed, contains the state seal in the center.

State Motto
Alki

The state motto is a Chinook Indian word meaning "By and by." It appeared on the territorial seal designed by Lieutenant J. K. Duncan.

In 1788, Captain John Meares named this range the Olympic Mountains because he felt the peaks were fit to house the gods.

BRITISH COLUMBIA
Ferndale
Bellingham
OKANOGAN NATIONAL FOREST
NORTH CASCADES NATIONAL PARK
MAKAH INDIAN RESERVATION
COLVILLE INDIAN RESERVATION
Port Angeles
Everett
OLYMPIC NATIONAL PARK
Puget Sound
WENATCHEE NATIONAL FOREST
Seattle
QUINAULT INDIAN RESERVATION
WASHINGTON
Wenatchee
Tacoma
PACIFIC OCEAN
Hoquiam
Aberdeen
Olympia
Cle Elum
Moses Lake
Ellensburg
MOUNT RAINIER NATIONAL PARK
Yakima
Snake
GIFFORD PINCHOT NATIONAL FOREST
YAKIMA INDIAN RESERVATION
Richland
Pasco
Kennewick
Longview
Kelso
Columbia River
Vancouver
MARYHILL
N
OREGON
State Capital
Cities or towns
OF SPECIAL INTEREST
0 10 20 40 60 80 100 120 Miles
0 10 20 40 60 80 100 120 140 160 180 200 Kilometres

Washington

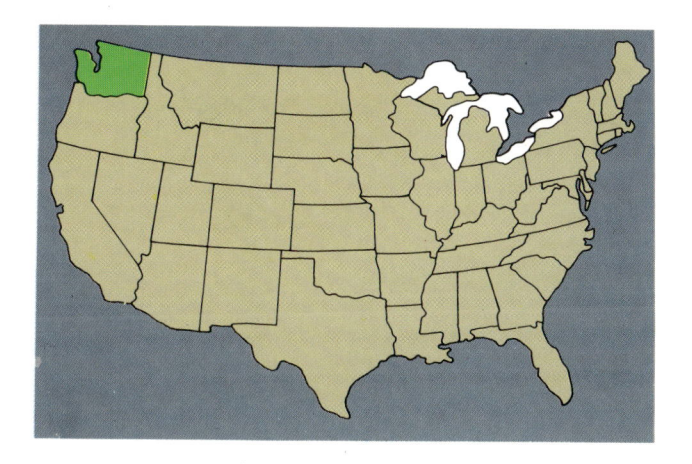

The Washington State Capitol is a part of the Capitol Way, a complex of buildings which includes the Legislative Building, the Governor's Mansion, the Temple of Justice, and the Washington State Library.

State Capital

Olympia became the territorial capital in 1855 and continued as the state capital after 1889. Construction on the present capitol building, designed by Ernest Flagg, began in 1919 and was completed in 1928. Built of Wilkeson sandstone, the 22-story structure cost $6,798,596. The dome, the fifth largest in the world, rises 287 feet and is topped by the "Lantern of Liberty." Doric columns surround the building, while Corinthian columns can be seen at the main north entrance and the south portico.

State Name and Nickname

The state of Washington was named for George Washington, the first president of the United States.

The official nickname of the state is the *Evergreen State* because of its many large fir and pine trees. Another nickname, no longer used, is the *Chinook State*, referring to the salmon industry and to the Chinook Indians.

State Flower

The western rhododendron, *Rhododendron macrophyllum*, was designated state flower in 1949.

State Tree

In 1947, the western hemlock, *Tsuga heterophylla*, was selected as state tree.

State Bird

The willow goldfinch, *Astragalinus tristis salicamans*, was adopted as state bird in 1951.

State Dance

The square dance was chosen state dance in 1979.

State Fish

In 1969, the Steelhead trout, *Salmo gairdnerii*, was named state fish.

State Gem

Petrified wood was adopted as state gem in 1975.

State Song

"Washington My Home," words and music by Helen Davis, was chosen state song in 1959.

Population

The population of Washington in 1990 was 4,887,941, making it the 18th most populous state. There are 71.7 people per square mile—73.5 percent of the population live in towns and cities.

Geography and Climate

Bounded by British Columbia on the north, Idaho on the east, Oregon on the south, and the Pacific Ocean on the west, Washington has an area of 68,139 square miles, making it the 20th largest state. The climate is mild, influenced by winds from the Pacific Ocean. Washington's six main land regions include the Olympic Mountains on the northwest peninsula, open land along the coast, flat terrain in the Puget Sound Lowland, the Cascade Mountains to the east of Puget Sound, the Columbia Basin in the central portion of the state, and the Rocky Mountains in the northeast. The highest point in the state, at 14,410 feet, is Mount Rainier in Pierce County, and the lowest point is at sea level along the Pacific Ocean and Puget Sound. The major waterways of the state are the Chehalis, Columbia, Colville, Cowlitz, Methow, Okanogan, Pend Oreille, Puyallup, Sanpoil, Skagit, Skykomish, Snake, Spokane, Wenatchee, and Yakima rivers. Franklin D. Roosevelt Lake, the largest in the state, is formed by the Grand Coulee Dam.

Washington

Industries

The principal industries of the state are aerospace, forest products, food products, primary metals, and agriculture. The chief manufactured products are aircraft, pulp and paper, lumber and plywood, aluminum, and processed fruits and vegetables.

Agriculture

The chief crops of the state are hops, spearmint oil, raspberries, apples, asparagus, pears, cherries, peppermint oil, and potatoes. Washington is also a livestock state. There are estimated to be 1.3 million cattle, 50,000 hogs and pigs, 59,000 sheep, and 5.7 million chickens and turkeys on its farms. Douglas fir, hemlock, cedar, and pine are harvested. Construction sand and gravel, crushed stone, and Portland cement are important mineral products. Commercial fishing brings in $134.6 million per year.

Government

The governor is elected for a four-year term, as are the lieutenant governor, secretary of state, treasurer, auditor, attorney general, superintendent of public instruction, commissioner of public lands, and insurance commissioner. The state legislature, which meets annually, consists of a 49-member senate and a 98-member house of representatives. Each of the 49 legislative districts elects one senator and two representatives. Senators serve four-year terms, while representatives serve two-year terms. The present constitution, adopted in 1889, has been amended more than 60 times. In addition to its two United States senators, Washington has nine representatives in the U.S.

14,410-foot Mount Rainier was named by George Vancouver for his friend Peter Rainier.

Fort Vancouver was once the center of the fur-trade on the Pacific Coast, and was Britain's last stronghold in the Pacific Northwest.

House of Representatives. The state has eleven votes in the electoral college.

History

Many Indians inhabited the Washington region before the arrival of the Europeans. The plateau Indian group, which included the Cayuse, Colville, Nez Percé, Okinagan, Spokane, and Yakima, lived east of the Cascade Mountains. The coastal Indians, which included the Chinook, Clallam, Clatsop, Nisqually, Nooksack, and Puyallup, occupied the land west of the Cascades.

Although Spanish and English sailors saw the region in the 1500s, the area that is now Washington was not explored until the late 1700s. In 1775, Spanish explorers Bruno Heceta and Juan Francisco de la Bodega y Quadra landed near present-day Point Grenville, claiming the region for Spain. England's claim to the area was based on the voyages of Captain James Cook in 1778 and of Captain George Vancouver, who explored and mapped the coastline in the early 1790s. In 1792, an American expedition led by Captain Robert Gray reached the mouth of the Columbia River. This discovery, together with the explorations of Meriwether Lewis and William Clark in 1805, accounted for the United States' claim to the region.

British and American fur traders were the first whites to settle in the area. In 1810, the Canadian North West Company built Spokane House, a trading post, near present-day Spokane. In 1811, Fort Okanogan was founded by a group of settlers sent by American fur trader John Jacob Astor. This was the first permanent American settlement on Washington soil.

At the outbreak of the War of 1812, Astor's company abandoned its trading posts. After the war, the United States and Great Britain, unable to agree on a boundary line between their territories, signed a treaty by which citizens of both countries were allowed to live and trade in the region. By the 1840s, many Americans had moved into the Oregon Territory, which included Washington. A boundary line was finally settled upon in 1846, when President James K. Polk signed a treaty with Great Britain.

When Washington became a territory in 1853, it included the present state of Washington, northern Idaho, and western Montana. In 1859, the southern parts of Idaho and Wyoming were incorporated into the territory. Washington's present boundaries were determined in 1863, when Congress created the Idaho Territory. The discovery of gold in Idaho, Oregon, and British Columbia brought many settlers to the region after 1860. The population increased again upon the completion of the Northern Pacific Railroad in 1883. On November 11, 1889, Washington was admitted to the Union as the 42nd state.

By 1900, agriculture, lumbering, fishing, and mining had become important to Washington's economy. Shipping developed as a major industry, and the port of Seattle prospered, aided by the Klondike and Alaska gold rushes.

During World War I, Puget Sound became a major shipbuilding center, and military installations expanded. After the war, the need for ships and war supplies decreased and many jobs were lost. This, combined with the Great Depression of the 1930s, dealt a harsh blow to the state's economy. The construction of the Bonneville and Grand Coulee dams during the late 1930s helped Washington begin its recovery. Prosperity returned when the United States entered World War II and Washington's industries again manufactured aircraft and ships for the war effort. Today, the state has become a leader in aircraft production, with the Boeing Company making its home in Seattle.

Sports

Many sporting events on the collegiate and secondary school levels are played throughout the state. In football, the University of Washington won the Rose Bowl in 1960, 1961, 1978, 1982, and 1991, and the Orange Bowl in 1985. Washington State University was triumphant in the Rose Bowl in 1916. The University of Washington has also been strong in the sport of rowing, with its women's team winning the Collegiate Varsity Eights championship in 1981, 1982, 1983, 1984,

1985, 1987, and 1988, and the men's team winning in 1984. In baseball, the team from Kirkland won the Little League World Series in 1982.

On the professional level, the Seattle Mariners of the American League play baseball in the Kingdome, which they share with the Seattle Seahawks of the National Football League. The Seattle SuperSonics of the National Basketball Association play their home games in the Coliseum.

Major Cities

Seattle (population 502,200). Founded in 1852 and named for a local Indian chief, Seattle is located on a narrow strip of land between Puget Sound and Lake Washington. About 2,000 ocean-going cargo ships visit this busy port each year. Much of its modern skyline owes its existence to the Century 21 Exposition of 1962.

Things to see in Seattle: Blake Island Marine State Park, Burke Museum, Center for Wooden Boats, Coast Guard Museum Northwest, Discovery Park, Ellis Park, Evergreen Point Floating Bridge, Fire Station No. 5, Fishermen's Terminal, Frye Museum, Henry Art Gallery, Kingdome, Lake Washington Ship Canal and Hiram M. Chittenden Locks, Museum of Flight, Museum of History and Industry, Nordic Heritage Museum, Pier 59, Seattle Aquarium, Fun Forest Amusement Park, Pacific Science Center, Seattle Children's Museum, Space Needle, Smith Tower, University of Washington Arboretum, Volunteer Park, Seattle Art Museum, Waterfront Park, Wing Luke Asian Museum, and Woodland Park Zoological Gardens.

Spokane (population 170,900). Settled in 1871, the city began as a sawmill at Spokane Falls. The coming of the railroads, along with the Idaho gold rush, sparked the city's growth. Despite suffering a devastating fire in

Seattle's Space Needle is just one of the many buildings that grace the city's skyline.

Washington

The Grand Coulee Dam was built during the Great Depression, under President Franklin D. Roosevelt's plan to provide much-needed jobs with public projects. The dam is now one of the world's largest hydroelectric engineering works.

1889, Spokane has developed into the largest railroad center west of Omaha and has become the economic and cultural center of the region.
Things to see in Spokane: Cathedral of St. John, Cheney Cowles Memorial Museum, Crosby Library, John A. Finch Arboretum, Manito Park, Mount Spokane, Museum of Native American Cultures, Riverfront Park, Splashdown Waterslide Park, Spokane House Interpretive Center, and Walk in the Wild.

Places to Visit

The National Park Service maintains 10 areas in the state of Washington: Olympic National Park, Mount Rainier National Park, North Cascades National Park, Fort Vancouver National Historic Site, Whitman Mission National Historic Site, Ross Lake National Recreation Area, Lake Chelan National Recreation Area, Coulee Dam National Recreation Area, San Juan Island National Historical Park, and Klondike Gold Rush National Historical Park. In addition, there are 86 state recreation areas.

Bellingham: Whatcom Museum of History and Art. Housed in the former city hall, this museum features logging industry memorabilia, and changing art exhibits.

Black Diamond: Black Diamond Historical Museum. This museum contains replicas of a western jail and a country doctor's office among its exhibits.

Cle Elum: Cle Elum Historical Telephone Museum. This museum displays old telephones, switchboards, and other equipment.

Coulee Dam: Grand Coulee Dam. One of the largest concrete structures in the world, the dam provides electric power for the region.

Eatonville: Northwest Trek. Visitors may ride a tram through the 600-acre wildlife preserve which contains moose, caribou, elk, and other animals in their natural surroundings.

Ferndale: Hovander Homestead. This restored 1903 homestead includes a barn, milkhouse, and children's farm zoo.

Hoquiam: Hoquiam's "Castle." This turreted 20-room mansion, the former home of lumber tycoon Robert Lytle, is furnished with many antiques.

Ilwaco: Lewis and Clark Interpretive Center. The center details the two-and-a-half-year, 8,000-mile journey of Meriwether Lewis and William Clark.

Neah Bay: Makah Cultural and Research Center. The museum contains over 55,000 artifacts of the Makah and Northwest Coast Indians, some dating back 2,000 years.

Olympia: State Capitol Museum. Originally the home of Olympia mayor Clarence Lord, the museum contains exhibits pertaining to the government of Washington.

Omak: St. Mary's Mission. Founded by Father Etienne de Rougé in 1886, the mission stands next to Paschal Sherman Indian School, the only Indian boarding school in Washington.

Puyallup: Ezra Meeker Mansion. Built in 1890, this 17-room Victorian mansion was the home of the town's first mayor.

Richland: Hanford Science Center. This museum focuses on energy through hands-on exhibits and computerized games.

Sequim: Olympic Game Farm. This 90-acre preserve is home to many of the animals that appear in wildlife films and television.

Tacoma: Point Defiance Park. The 700-acre park features Fort Nisqually, Never Never Land, Point Defiance Zoo and Aquarium, and the Natural Habitat Aviary.

Events

There are many events and organizations that schedule activities of various kinds in the state of Washington. Here are some of them.

Sports: Rodeo Days (Cheney), Ellensburg Rodeo (Ellensburg), Silver Lake Triathlon (Everett), Scottish Highland Games (Ferndale), Capital City Marathon and Relay (Olympia), Omak Stampede and Suicide Race (Omak), Goodwill Games (Seattle), horseracing at Longacres Race Course (Seattle), Loggerodeo (Sedro Woolley), Diamond Spur Rodeo (Spokane), Lilac Bloomsday Run (Spokane).

Arts and Crafts: National Western Art Show and Auction (Ellensburg), Living Museum (Ephrata), Ezra Meeker Community Festival (Puyallup), Sunfest (Richland), Pacific Northwest Arts and Crafts Fair (Seattle), Western Art Show and Auction (Spokane).

Music: Mountaineers' Forest Theater (Bremerton), Jazz Unlimited (Pasco), Pacific Northwest Ballet (Seattle), Seattle Symphony (Seattle), Opera House and Convention Center (Spokane), Spokane Symphony (Spokane), Tacoma Symphony Orchestra (Tacoma).

Entertainment: Asotin County Fair (Asotin), Apple Days (Cashmere), King County Fair (Enumclaw), Salty Sea Days (Everett), Washington State International Air Fair (Everett), Fall Foliage Festival (Federal Way), Old Settlers Pioneer Days Picnic (Ferndale), Ski to Sea Festival (Ferndale), Yakima Valley Junior Fair (Grandview), Christmas Lighting Festival (Leavenworth), Maifest (Leavenworth), Washington State Autumn Leaf Festival (Leavenworth), Strawberry Festival (Marysville), Loggers Jubilee (Morton), Skagit Valley Tulip Festival (Mount Vernon), Makah Days (Neah Bay), Holland Happening (Oak

Washington

Harbor), Capitol Lakefair (Olympia), Harbor Days (Olympia), Sunflower Festival (Omak), Rhododendron Festival (Port Townsend), Skandia Midsommarfest (Poulsbo), Vikingfest (Poulsbo), Yule Log Festival (Poulsbo), Daffodil Festival (Puyallup), Western Washington State Fair (Puyallup), Heritage Festival (Redmond), Bumbershoot (Seattle), Harvest Festival (Seattle), Northwest Folklife Festival (Seattle), Norwegian Constitution Day (Seattle), Seattle Seafair (Seattle), Irrigation Festival (Sequim), West Coast Oyster Shucking Contest (Shelton), Evergreen State Fair (Snohomish), Interstate Fair (Spokane), Lilac Festival (Spokane), Toppenish Creek Encampment (Toppenish), Apple Blossom Festival (Wenatchee), Lilac Festival (Woodland), Central Washington Fair (Yakima).

Tours: Boeing 747-767 Division (Everett), Victorian Homes Tour (Port Townsend), Seattle Harbor Tour (Seattle), Annual Homes Tour (Snohomish), Tacoma Harbor Tour (Tacoma).

Theater: Laughing Horse Summer Theatre (Ellensburg), A Contemporary Theater (Seattle), Bagley Wright Theatre (Seattle), 5th Avenue Theatre (Seattle), The Indian Dinner Theatre (Seattle), Intiman at the Seattle Center Playhouse (Seattle), Omnidome Film Experience (Seattle), IMAX Theatre (Spokane), Spokane Civic Theatre (Spokane).

Two women participate in the log-rolling competition at the Loggers Jubilee.

Famous People

Many famous people were born in the state of Washington. Here are a few:

Earl Anthony b. 1930, Kent. Champion bowler

Earl Averill 1902-83, Snohomish. Hall of Fame baseball player

Mildred Bailey 1907-51, Tekoa. Jazz singer

Howard Blakeslee 1880-1952, New Dungeness. Science writer and editor

Bobby Brown b. 1924, Seattle. Baseball player and American League president

Scott Buchanan 1895-1968, Sprague. Philosopher and educator

Dyan Cannon b. 1937,

Tacoma. Film actress: *Bob and Carol and Ted and Alice*

Chester F. Carlson 1906-68, Seattle. Physicist and inventor of xerography

Joanne Carner b. 1939, Kirkland. Champion golfer

Horace Cayton 1903-70, Seattle. Sociologist and author

Ron Cey b. 1948, Tacoma. Baseball player

Carol Channing b. 1921, Seattle. Stage actress: *Gentlemen Prefer Blondes, Hello Dolly!*

Judy Collins b. 1939, Seattle. Folk singer

Bing Crosby 1904-77, Tacoma. Singer and Academy Award-winning film actor: *Going My Way, High Society*

Constance Cummings b. 1910, Seattle. Tony Award-winning actress: *Wings*

Merce Cunningham b. 1919, Centralia. Choreographer

Glen Edwards 1907-73, Mold. Football player

Daniel J. Evans b. 1925, Seattle. Governor of Washington

Muir Fairchild 1894-1950, Bellingham. Army and air force officer in World War I

Frederick Faust 1892-1944, Seattle. Novelist: *The Untamed, Destry Rides Again*

Spokane Garry 1811-92, Spokane County. Indian leader

Jimi Hendrix 1942-70, Seattle. Rock guitarist

Frank Herbert 1920-86, Tacoma. Novelist: *Dune, Dragon in the Sea*

Bob Houbregs b. 1932, Seattle. Hall of Fame basketball player

Fred Hutchinson 1919-64, Seattle. Baseball manager

Henry Jackson 1912-83, Everett. Senate leader

Robert Joffrey 1930-88, Seattle. Choreographer

Dudley Knox 1877-1960, Walla Walla. Naval officer and historian

Leschi ?-1858, near the Nisqually River. Indian leader

Karl Llewellyn 1893-1962, West Seattle. Legal philosopher and educator

Kenny Loggins b. 1948, Everett. Pop singer

Phil Mahre b. 1957, White Pass. Ski champion

Kevin McCarthy b. 1914, Seattle. Film actor: *Invasion of the Body Snatchers, A Gathering of Eagles*

Mary McCarthy 1912-89,

Bing Crosby, was one of the leading American singers for three decades, from the 1930s to the 1950s, and was a popular movie star as well.

Seattle. Novelist and critic: *The Group, Memories of a Catholic Girlhood*
Guthrie McClintic 1893-1961, Seattle. Theatrical producer and director
Robert Motherwell 1915-1991, Aberdeen. Artist
Patrice Munsel b. 1925, Spokane. Operatic singer
Randy Myers b. 1962, Vancouver. Baseball pitcher
Gene Nelson b. 1920, Seattle. Dancer and film actor: *The West Point Story, Oklahoma!*
Janis Paige b. 1922, Tacoma. Film and stage actress: *Please Don't Eat the Daisies, The Pajama Game*
Clyde Pangborn 1894-1958, Bridgeport. Aviator
Dixy Lee Ray b. 1914, Tacoma. Governor and head of U.S. Atomic Energy Commission
Jimmie Rodgers b. 1933, Camas. Pop singer
Ryne Sandberg b. 1959, Spokane. Baseball player
Ron Santo b. 1940, Seattle. Baseball player
John Stockton b. 1962, Spokane. Basketball player
Robert Stroud 1890-1963, Seattle. Ornithologist known as "The Bird Man of Alcatraz"
Genevieve Taggard 1894-1948, Waitsburg. Poet: *Travelling Standing Still*
Audrey-May Wurdemann 1911-60, Seattle. Pulitzer Prize-winning poet: *Bright Ambush*

Colleges and Universities
There are many colleges and universities in Washington. Here are the more prominent, with their locations, dates of founding, and enrollments.
Central Washington University, Ellensburg, 1891, 7,109
Eastern Washington University, Cheney, 1890, 8,098
Evergreen State College, Olympia, 1967, 3,237
Gonzaga University, Spokane, 1887, 3,840
Pacific Lutheran University, Tacoma, 1890, 3,855
Seattle Pacific University, Seattle, 1891, 3,435
Seattle University, Seattle, 1892, 4,510
University of Puget Sound, Tacoma, 1888, 3,303
University of Washington, Seattle, 1861, 33,238
Walla Walla College, College Place, 1892, 1,581
Washington State University, Pullman, 1890, 17,138
Western Washington University, Bellingham, 1893, 9,322
Whitman College, Walla Walla, 1859, 1,268
Whitworth College, Spokane, 1890, 1,788

Where To Get More Information
Travel Development Division
Dept. of Commerce and Economic Development
General Administration Bldg.
Olympia, WA 98504

Bibliography

General

Aylesworth, Thomas G. and Virginia L. *Let's Discover the States: The Northwest*. New York: Chelsea House, 1988.

Alaska

Alaska: High Roads to Adventure. DC: National Geographic Society, 1976.

Carpenter, Allan. *Alaska*, rev. ed. Chicago: Childrens Press, 1979.

Fradin, Dennis B. *Alaska in Words and Pictures*. Chicago: Childrens Press, 1977.

Hunt, William R. *Alaska: A Bicentennial History*. New York: Norton, 1976.

Wheeler, Keith. *The Alaskans*. New York: Time, Inc., 1977.

Idaho

Beal, Merrill D., and Merle W. Wells. *History of Idaho*. 3 vols. New York: Lewis Historical Publishing Company, 1959.

Carpenter, Allan. *Idaho*, rev. ed. Chicago: Childrens Press, 1979.

Fradin, Dennis B. *Idaho in Words and Pictures*. Chicago: Childrens Press, 1980.

Jensen, Dwight W. *Discovering Idaho: A History*. Caldwell, ID: Caxton, 1977.

Peterson, Frank Ross. *Idaho: A Bicentennial History*. New York: Norton, 1976.

Wells, Merle W., and Arthur A. Hart. *Idaho, Gem of the Mountains*. Northridge, CA: Windsor Publications, 1985.

Young, Virgil M. *The Story of Idaho*. Moscow: University Press of Idaho, 1977.

Oregon

Carpenter, Allan. *Oregon*, rev. ed. Chicago: Childrens Press, 1979.

Clark, Malcolm, Jr. *Eden Seekers: The Settlement of Oregon, 1818-1862*. Boston: Houghton Mifflin, 1981.

Dodds, Gordon B. *Oregon: A Bicentennial History*. New York: Norton, 1977.

Fradin, Dennis B. *Oregon in Words and Pictures*. Chicago: Childrens Press, 1980.

Thollander, Earl. *Back Roads of Oregon*. New York: Crown, 1979.

Washington

Atkeson, Ray A. *A Portrait of Washington*. Portland, OR: Graphic Arts Center, 1980.

Avery, Mary W. *Washington: A History of the Evergreen State*, rev. ed. Seattle: University of Washington Press, 1965.

Carpenter, Allan. *Washington*, rev. ed. Chicago: Childrens Press, 1979.

Clark, Norman H. *Washington: A Bicentennial History*. New York: Norton, 1976.

Fradin, Dennis B. *Washington in Words and Pictures*. Chicago: Childrens Press, 1980.

Index

A
Adelman, Rick, *40*
Aleuts, 12
Alsek River, 11
Anchorage (AK), 14-15, *15*
Astor, John Jacob, 39, 54, 55
Astoria (OR), 39
Athapaskan Indians, 12

B
Bannock Indians, 25, 26, 38
Baranof, Alexander, 12, 13
Barnette, E. T., 15
Bear River, 25
Benson, Benny, 7
Bering, Vitus, 12
Boise (ID), 23, 27
Bonneville Dam, 40, 55
Borah Peak, 25
Buchanan, J. A., 37
Bush, Asahel, II, *38*

C
Capitol Way, *51*
Cayuse Indians, 38, 54
Chehalis River, 52
Chief Buffalo Horn, 26
Chief Joseph, 26
Chinook Indians, 38, 49, 52, 54
Civil War, 39
Clackama Indians, 38
Clallam Indians, 54
Clark, William, 26, 39, 54
Clatsop Indians, 54
Clearwater River, 25, 26
Coeur d'Alene Indians, 25
Coliseum, the, 56
Columbia River, 36, 37, 38, 39, 40, 52, 54
Colville Indians, 54
Colville River, 11, 52
Cook, James, 12, 38, 54
Copper River, 11, 13
Cowlitz River, 52
Crater Lake, *32*, 37
Crosby, Bing, *60*

D
Davis, Helen, 52
de la Bodega y Quadra, Juan Francisco, 54
Deschutes River, 37
Dolly Wares Museum, *42*
Douglas, Sally Hume, 24
Drake, Marie, 10
Drake, Sir Francis, 38
Duncan, J.K., 49
Dusenbury, Elinor, 10

E
Ellerhusen, Ulric, H., 35
Eskimos, 12
Events: Arts and Crafts (AK), 18; (ID), 28; (OR), 43; (WA), 58; Entertainment (AK), 18; (ID), 29; (OR), 44; (WA), 58-59; Music (AK), 18; (ID), 28-29; (OR), 43-44; (WA), 58; Sports (AK), 17; (ID), 28; (OR), 42-43; (WA), 58; Theater (AK), 18; (ID), 29; (OR), 44; (WA), 59; Tours (AK), 18; (ID), 29; (OR), 44; (WA), 59

F
Fairbanks (AK), 15
Flagg, Ernest, 51
Fort Boise (ID), 26
Fort Hall (ID), 26
Fort Okanogan, 54
Fort Vancouver, 39, *54*
Franklin (ID), 26
Franklin D. Roosevelt Lake, 52

G
Glacier Bay (AK), *6*
Grand Coulee Dam, 55, *57*
Gray, Robert, 38, 54
Great Depression, 13, 27, 39, 55, *57*
Green, Emma Edwards, 19

H
Haida Indians, 12
Harris, Richard, 13
Heceta, Bruno, 54
Helm, McKinley, 24
Historic Bush House, *38*

I
Idaho Falls, 27
Iliamna Lake, 11
Indian Wars, 39

J
John Day River, 37
Juneau (AK), 9, 13
Juneau, Joe, 13

K
Keally, Francis, 35
Ketchikan (AK), *16*
Ketchum (ID), *29*
Kingdome, 56
Klamath Indians, 38
Klondike River, 13
Kobuk River, 11
Koyukuk River, 11
Kuskokwim River, 11
Kutenai Indians, 25

L
Lake Washington, 56
Lee, Jason, 41
Lewis, Meriwether, 26, 39, 54
Lewiston (ID), 23
Loggers Jubilee, *59*

M
Matanuska River, 11
McLoughlin, John, 39
Meares, John, *48*
Memorial Coliseum, 41
Methow River, 52
Modoc Indians, 38
Mormons, 26
Mount Hood, 37
Mount Mazama, *32*
Mount McKinley, 11
Mount Rainier, 52, *53*
Mount Saint Elias, 12
Multnomah Indians, 38
Murtagh, Henry B., 37

N
Nez Percé National Historic Park, *20*
Nez Percé Indians, 25, 26, 38, 54, *54*
Noatak River, 11
Nome (AK), 13
Nooksack Indians, 54

O
Okanogan Indians, 54
Okanogan River, 52
Olympia (WA), 51
Olympic Mountains, *48*
Omaha (NE), 27
Organic Act, 13
Orofino Creek, 26

Index

P
Paiute Indians, 38
Payette River, 25
Pend d'Oreille Indians, 25
Pend Oreille Lake, 26
Pend Oreille River, 52
Peter the Great, 12
Peter, Richard, 7
Pettygrove, Francis, 41
Pocatello (ID), 27
Point Grenville (WA), 54
Polk, James K., 39, 55
Portland (OR), 27, 40, 41
Portland Trail Blazers, *40*, 41
Powell, Jane, *45*
Prudhoe Bay (AK), 14, *14*
Puget Sound, 55, 56
Puyallup Indians, 54
Puyallup River, 52

R
Rainier, Peter, *53*
Rend Oreille Lake, 25
Roosevelt, Franklin D., *57*

S
Salem (OR), 41
Salmon River, 25
Sanpoil River, 52
Sarpi, Pietro, 21
Seattle (WA), 55, 56, *56*
Seattle Mariners, 56
Seattle Seahwaks, 56
Seattle SuperSonics, 56
Seward, William H., 10, 13
Shelikof, 12

Shoshone Indians, 24, 25
Sitka (AK), 12
Skagit River, 52
Skykomish River, 52
Snake River, 25, 26, 37, 52
Space Needle, *56*
Spalding, Henry H., 26
Spokane (WA), 56-57
Spokane Falls, 56
Spokane Indians, 54
Spokane River, 52
State animal (OR), 36
State bird (AK), 10, *10*; (ID), 24; (OR), 36, *36*; (WA), 52
State capital (AK), 9, *9*; (ID), 23, *23*; (OR), 35, *35*; (WA), 51, *51*
State dance (OR), 36; (WA), 52
State fish (AK), 10; (OR), 36; (WA), 52
State flag (AK), 7; (ID), 21; (OR), 33; (WA), 49
State flower (AK), 10, *10*; (ID), 24, *24*; (OR), 36, *36*; (WA), 52
State gem (AK), 10; (ID), 24; (WA), 52
State gemstone (OR), 36
State horse (ID), 24
State hostess (OR), 36
State insect (OR), 37
State marine mammal (AK), 10
State mineral (AK), 10
State motto (AK), 7; (ID), 21; (OR), 33; (WA), 49
State rock (OR), 37
State seal (AK), 5, *5*; (ID), 19, *19*; (OR), 31, *31*; (WA), 47, *47*
State song (AK), 10; (ID), 24; (OR), 37; (WA), 52
State sport (AK), 10
State tree (AK), 10; (ID), 24; (OR), 36; (WA), 52

Steunenberg, Frank, 26
Stikine River, 11
Susitna River, 11
Taku River, 11
Tanana River, 11
Thompson, David, 26
Tillamook Indians, 38
Tlingit Indians, 12, *16*
Tompkins, Albert J., 24
Tsimashian Indians, 12

U
Umatilla Indians, 38

V
Valdez (AK), 14
Vancouver, George, *6*, 39, *53*, 54

W
War of 1812, 55
Washington D.C., *23*
Washington, George, 47, 52
Wenatchee River, 52
White Bird Canyon (ID), 26
Willamette River, 37, 41
Willing, Geroge M., 24
World War I, 26, 55
World War II, 14, 27, 40, 55

Y
Yakima Indians, 54
Yakima River, 52
Yellowstone National Park, *26*
Yukon River, 11

Photo Credits/Acknowledgments

Photos on pages 3 (top), 5-7, 9, 10 (top, Ernst Schneider, bottom, Stoughton), 11, 13-17, courtesy of Alaska Division of Tourism; pages 3 (middle), 19, courtesy Idaho Secretary of State; pages 21, 23-24, courtesy of Idaho Travel Council; pages 3 (bottom), 31, 35-36, courtesy of Oregon Tourism Division; pages 4, 47, courtesy of Washington Secretary of State; pages 48-49, 51, 53-54, 57, 59, courtesy of State of Washington Tourism Division; pages 20-21 (Woodbridge Williams), 26 (Stoughton), 32-33, courtesy of National Park Service; page 29, courtesy of Michael Guryan; page 33, courtesy of Oregon Economic Development Department; page 38, courtesy of Historic Bush House (Zane Holland); page 40, courtesy of Portland Trail Blazers (Brian Drake); page 42 courtesy of Dolly Wares Doll Museum; page 43, courtesy of Salem Art Festival; pages 45, 60, courtesy of Movie Material Store; page 56, courtesy of Seattle-King County News Bureau.

Cover photograph courtesy of Alaska Division of Tourism.

Foreword

We are grateful to be able to bring into English print for the first time this moving story from the days of the Reformation in the Netherlands (1556-1566). In these pages the vivid reality of vital Christianity shines lustrously. Oh, that God Himself would revive us with the kind of courage to suffer persecution willingly for His Name's sake as abounds in this story! Here you will see Matthew 5:11-12 graphically illustrated: "Blessed are ye, when men shall revile you, and persecute you, and shall say all manner of evil against you falsely, for My sake. Rejoice, and be exceeding glad: for great is your reward in heaven: for so persecuted they the prophets which were before you."

The Inquisitor's Secretary is an excellent story also for teenagers to read. It is our prayer that God may bless this little volume for the spiritual well-being of young and old.

*Netherlands Reformed Book
and Publishing Committee*